SCS

What Every Artist Needs to Know About

paints
&
colors

David Pyle

Published by

krause
publications

700 E. State St., Iola, WI 54990-0001

Please call or write for our free catalog of publications. Our toll-free number to place an order or obtain a free catalog is 800-258-0929 or please use our regular business telephone 715-445-2214 for editorial comment and further information.

Library of Congress Catalog Number 99-69484
ISBN 0-87341-831-X

Dedication

To Jordan and Christopher, in the hopes that they are able to find the same measure of joy, passion, and pleasure that has been given to their father, who has been blessed to work with the extraordinary people and products that make up the art materials community.

Acknowledgments

A couple of years ago, I had the opportunity to share a dinner table with Christo and Jeanne-Claude, the husband and wife artist team that has changed the face of late-twentieth century art with their Rifle Gap Valley Curtain, fabric-wrapped Reichstag in Berlin, and Umbrellas project in California and Japan. I was preparing to write a feature article on the pair and, in the hopes of setting up a later interview, had managed to finagle a dinner invitation following one of their many speaking engagements.

Way beyond midnight, after finishing a full meal—and well past the point where the conversation had veered away from art and was focused upon our children—Jeanne-Claude leaned toward me and quietly said, "Doing what you want is easy. Knowing what you want is the hard part."

For a few moments, I couldn't say anything; her comment had rocked me like an earthquake. As casually as if she'd mentioned that the weather was nice, she'd said something that I'd been struggling with for most of my life. I couldn't sleep that night, and her words have continued to echo in my head over the last year.

I spent months after that dinner trying to find an answer to that fundamental question: What do I want? And this book—along with the other activities that currently keep me busy—was set in motion by that comment from Jeanne-Claude. It became clear that, as much as I care about the community that makes and uses art materials, I needed to find some vehicle to articulate a few important issues. Hence, this volume.

As with any enterprise requiring this much information, a great deal of credit is due to many different people. And it's only fair to say that all of the information in this book that is accurate is the result of the expertise and dedication from many individuals, while any mistakes or misinformation is of my doing, alone.

To Alun Foster and Emma Pearce, probably the most art-materials knowledgeable husband and wife team on the planet, I owe a great debt, not only for their patient review of the manuscript, but for their time over the years in helping me better understand the mechanics of paint and color.

To Steve Pleune and Richard Goodban of ColArt/Winsor & Newton, for their support and interest in helping me complete this project, not to mention their tolerance of my professional quirks and my insistence over the years upon wearing a Winsor & Newton brush upon my head. To Lynn Pearl of Winsor & Newton for her friendship and support.

To Robert and Martha Gamblin, as well as to Mark and Barbara Golden, along with Anthony Sorosky, for their grace and willingness to help someone who sometimes has been required to don a "competitive" hat. To Howard and Kathryn Clark, of Twinrocker Paper, for providing me with a model of dedication to one's art and craft, not to mention the loveliest paper that I've ever painted and drawn upon. To Laurie Hines, for great stories, terrific ideas, and careful proofing.

To Duane Slick at the Rhode Island School of Design for helping me better understand how environmental issues are evolving within this community. And to art material retailers like Beth Bergman, Linda Snelling, Bill Cavanagh, George Bussinger, Joe Teti, and others too numerous to name here, who have been my friends, confidants, and supporters for many years. To Mark Gottsegen for his unremitting and uncompromising passion for the products and how they are used. And to two individuals who have given of themselves with amazing zeal for decades, helping the community grow from infancy to maturity, Zora Sweet Pinney and Jean Bourges. I hope that I have half of their energy and enthusiasm when I arrive at those same later decades of my life.

To Henry and Candy Meininger, and to the memory of their father, "Cap," for the launching place they gave me within the community. And to a couple of extraordinary educators, Susan Josepher and Lon Seymour. I'm also greatly indebted to two young advisors, Devany and Anika, for helping me to remember that the things that are important in life at age forty aren't terribly different from those that are important at ages ten and thirteen.

I also owe a great debt to a number of very bright and insightful magazine editors: Mike Ward, Sandy Carpenter, Tina Manzer, and Karen Ancona. And to a remarkable magazine publisher, Jeff Lapin, who always has good things to say. Many thanks are also due to my patient and delightful book editors with Krause Publications: Amy Tincher-Durik and Don Gulbrandsen. And thank you to Stephen Doherty of American Artists for his willingness to review the manuscript.

And, for helping me to find the great pleasures that come in just putting the words on paper, I'm deeply grateful to Melissa Jory, Joey Porcelli, Diane Dunne, Ellen Wilensky, and the memory of Bernie Baker.

I'd be remiss if I didn't say thank you to all of the students, artists, and staff from stores and manufacturers who have asked great questions over the years. Every query has taken me someplace new and exciting.

And, of course, to Christo and Jeanne-Claude, for those words that still ring in my ears.

Finally, to my wife Tina, whose patience and love has been the greatest blessing imaginable; and for whom I wonder if I could have been half as patient if I were married to me.

Last but not least, I must acknowledge that some versions or portions of this text have appeared in *The Artist's Magazine* and *Art Materials Today* (F&W Publications), *CNA Magazine* (Krause Publications), *Art Materials Retailer* (Fahy Williams Publications), and within some communication vehicles written by the author for ColArt/Winsor & Newton. The author is deeply grateful to F&W Publications, Krause Publications, Fahy-Williams, and to ColArt for permission to reprint, in expanded or edited versions, these sections of text.

Table of Contents

Introduction
Who Needs This Book?

What are the biggest differences that a guy named Michelangelo (or Rembrandt or Vermeer) would notice if he were magically transported into a school or college art studio in the year 2000? Besides the novelty of air conditioning, the joys of disposable cups full of cappuccino and cola, and the clamorous music coming from strange little boxes with glowing numbers (radios), he'd be stunned by three truly revolutionary changes to the process of making art.

First, he'd be surprised that everyone is squeezing paint from little tubes. "Where is your paint muller?" he'd ask.

A paint muller is a heavy stone or glass handle in the shape of an oversized chess pawn that's used on a flat stone surface to mix pigment with binder into a fine suspension and make paint. Mulling fine artists' color takes untold skill and experience, along with no

Smalt pigment. The earliest of cobalt pigments, present in small quantities in Egyptian paintings. The color came into more common use in the fifteenth century, when the cobalt ore was roasted to create a cobalt oxide, which was then added to molten glass. The glass was poured into cold water, breaking the mass into tiny particles. Small particles of the ground glass gave a pale blue pigment, while the coarser pieces made for a deep purple-blue. Because of its nature as glass, the color was very transparent. Courtesy of Winsor & Newton.

small measure of muscle and sweat. Up until the nineteenth century—when the Industrial Revolution made it possible to produce large quantities of paint, and sell color and brushes and prepared surfaces through the local colourman shop—the studio of every self-respecting artist was equipped with a serviceable muller with which to grind his own color from raw materials.

Second, he'd be astonished at the number of people in the class. "You all take lessons from one teacher?" our time traveler would ask. "Why doesn't the artist just have a few *discepolo*—uh, how you say—apprentices? How many people are painting and sculpting in this crazy time? Shouldn't some of you be working on the plumbing or farming or killing chickens for dinner?"

Beginning in the nineteenth century (again, because of the Industrial Revolution), lots of people found that they had the time and inclination to give in to their artistic urges. Instead of apprenticing to an already established master—and spending hours grinding color and cupping brushes and preparing their master's painting surface—people wanting to paint found that they could buy the paints and brushes and other essentials and just do it. Soon, art schools began springing up all over, which led to art diplomas, which led to discount art catalogs, which led to more schools and even workshops for $2,000 a week in Italy and France, and then instructional magazines, and discount art material web sites, and, finally, more art videos than any artistic-type could watch in a lifetime.

Lastly, after talking at length with the students in the classroom, he'd be amazed—and certainly dismayed—at the lack of knowledge about how the materials are used. "Mama Mia! You're going to add all that solvent to the paint!?" he'd cry. "What will keep the color on the surface?"

There's no question that making art possible for virtually everyone has been a wonderful thing. But we've paid a price. We've lost a basic understanding and intimacy with how all of those glorious paints and pastels and colored pencils and papers and colored grounds can best be used. We no longer spend time mixing pigment with the vehicle and the binder, and then carefully mulling the mixture into glorious color and, in the process, developing an essential understanding of what makes that paint stay on the surface for longer than a week or two. We don't really know when to choose transparent colors over opaque. We've not yet figured out how to best make use of modern pigments, those high-powered, high-tinting colors that have funny names like phthalocyanine and benzimidazolone.

And it shows in our art. Even worse, it all too often shows in the dusting of color that lies upon the floor after falling from the surface of our paintings. This book is a modest step toward solving those challenges.

This book is for every art student and every painter who wants to enjoy the art-making process more than ever before. Because that's what the information within these pages will do: it will give you the

Gamboge, a tree resin from Cambodia. Used for centuries in Asia, and first imported to Europe in 1615. Courtesy of Winsor & Newton.

power to make great choices about your materials; informed choices that will make your process more successful. And if that ain't fun, I don't know what is.

So what about Michelangelo in the twenty-first century? After a short time, I'm sure he'd settle in just fine. He'd put on blue jeans and grab a tall Starbucks decaf-nonfat-caramel-macchiato. He'd shake his head and smile at being called "Mike" and then he'd pick up a brush or a chisel and leap into the creative fray. Then, one day, while wandering down the art school hallway, past a studio filled with strange, flickering light, he'd get a glimpse at images created on a computer. And—holy electronic Madonnas!—he'd have a gazillion fresh questions, and the world would turn upside down all over again.

Ink sacks from squid. Courtesy of Winsor & Newton.

Chapter 1

The Color of History, or What Colors Would Rembrandt Choose Today?

Let's get it out of the way at the very beginning. Anyone who knows me or my work knows that I can't resist illustrating a point here or a principle there by telling stories about my kids. I'll readily admit that I tell these tales, in large part, because I'm a sucker for my children. I also do it because young people, in addition to being full of wonder as fresh as first morning light, are the world's best teachers. There's nothing like spending time with a four-year-old to help you see the world anew. So, without further ado, and to keep anyone who knows me from wondering when the kid stories are going to surface, here's the first (and not the last) telling anecdote:

A few months ago I was playing in the yard with my then three-year-old daughter, Jordan, and my almost two-year-old son, Christopher. In the driveway were enough basketballs, remote-controlled trains, and tricycles to entertain an army of toddlers, an age demographic in which I sometimes feel as comfortable as my children. We live at the top of a substantial hill and, every few minutes, I found myself chasing one ball or another down the driveway in an attempt to keep it from reaching the street, where it surely would gain enough downhill momentum that it

Whole watercolor cakes, from 1865. Courtesy of Winsor & Newton.

wouldn't stop until it reached the rainwater-filled ditch that runs at the bottom of the slope. For some reason, the children think it's funny to watch their daddy galloping, yelling, and waving after a ball as it picks up speed toward lower elevations.

Huffing and puffing, I trudged back up the street, a red and black mini-basketball under my arm, and saw Jordan gathering dried stalks from the day-lilies that line the driveway. "What are you doing, sweetheart?" I hollered. Standing up, she waved the handful of amber-colored sticks in one hand and a few stones in another, and said, "I'm gettin' stuff for making art, Dad!"

After we got inside, Jordan sat down at her drawing table and began to work diligently on a drawing with crayons and pencils. Christopher peered over her shoulder as she pulled out a bottle of glue and carefully pasted her day-lily sticks, along a few other yard-objects, to the paper. Proudly clutching her creation, she marched up to me and announced, "Lookit all the things I can use to make art!"

Bells went off in my head; out of the mouths of babes, and all that. No matter how far we travel along the highway of "progress," passengers on the

8

technological turnpike, we somehow, some way, find ourselves coming full circle. While my daughter's use of day-lily stalks may be instructive, it's certainly not new.

There is magic in making art, a transformative quality that children understand instinctively. By its very nature, the process of making art demands that you learn something about yourself and, more important, that you learn something about who and what you can become.

For as long as we've been recording ideas and events as "history," and even before that, we have used anything we could get our hands on in the search for that transformative magic. It started with burnt sticks and charred bones and animal fat and saliva. Then we moved onto ground earth and stewed flowers and powdered mummies (no kidding!). That's just for painting and drawing, and doesn't count all of the metals and earthen clay and wood and found objects (like day-lilies) used for doing sculpture or other three-dimensional work.

By the early nineteenth century, chemistry had flowered as a science, and artists could choose from a new range of pigments and a wealth of creative opportunities, the likes of which had never before been seen. With those new colors, the Impressionists changed how we see the world. And that was just for starters.

True confessions time. When I first began this project, and did my initial outline for this chapter on the history of colors, I was looking for a few key pieces of evidence that would add some heft to the axe I was looking to grind. Since the early twentieth century, the development of new pigments, new mediums, and new vehicles has accelerated at a blinding pace. There are now more opportunities for creative expression, and better products for exploring those opportunities, than could have ever been dreamed by Michelangelo or Rembrandt or Monet or Matisse or even Picasso and Pollack and Warhol. I wanted to make the point that the people who make paints and colors and brushes and pencils and papers, as we turn the corner into this new millennium, are at their most razor sharp, that artists and creative-types can take advantage of the very best creative materials that have ever been produced.

In fact, as the project evolved, I was stunned. I've been an active part of the community that makes brushes, paints, and papers for almost twenty years. I've been in and out of factories and mills. I've read everything there is to read. I count among my friends some of the most creative, knowledgeable people in the industry, people from every continent on the planet. I knew that this is a community that makes good stuff, and I wanted to write about it. I quickly found, however, that I didn't know the half of it.

It soon became clear that today's paints and colors are so much better, and there are so many improved options for artists and creative-types, that there is virtually no comparison with the older incarnations. As my friend Emma Pearce, Technical Services Manager for Winsor & Newton in Wealdstone, England, says, "(Today's) artists work with colours produced by an industry that has spent two centuries getting better and better and better and better, while most people in this world have to work with things that have gotten worse and worse."

With that in mind, there are two simple premises, the understanding of which are absolutely essential before going further in this book. If necessary, close your eyes and repeat these precepts over and over. Write them on a piece of paper and tape it to the ceiling above your bed so they're the first things you see in the morning. The first is a statement, and the second is a question:

1. At the turn of the twenty-first century, artists' colors and tools are the very best, by a very wide margin, that have ever been produced, and

2. If Michelangelo or Rembrandt or Monet or Matisse were offered the tools that we have today, would they have painted the way they did?

As a group, we painters are more than a bit, um, intransigent. It took forty years for phthalocyanine blue to come to wide acceptance on the community paint palette. With all of the new colors and mediums and opportunities that are available, many of us still think of painting, and the mechanics required to make a painting, in terms of WWRD? (What Would Rembrandt Do?).

While I'm not here to cast any stones at Rembrandt, I have no doubt that he would have been staggered by the comparative differences in his color choices versus those available to the twentieth-century creative-type. Would he have painted in the same manner if he had today's tools? Who knows. He's not here to tell us; we can't send him an e-mail and ask for an interview.

This book isn't intended to make anybody stop painting like Rembrandt (or Michelangelo or Vermeer or Monet or Mondrian or Klee or Pollack or

Drying oils and gums. Fats, oils, waxes, gums, eggs, and now thermoplastic resins, have been used as vehicles for fine color. No matter what's used, the function of a vehicle is to carry, coat, and secure the pigment within a permanent film. Courtesy of Winsor & Newton.

Frankenthaler or O'Keefe). It's intended to help you understand your options and your opportunities. For, whether in the form of the transparent earth colors used by Rembrandt (because that's all he had), or a new medium that offers a previously impossible visual effect, or a new sparkling pigment, or even day-lily stalks from the garden, the opportunities for transformative magic are mighty, indeed.

We need a little context—a smattering of history—to fully understand what's waiting at our fingertips...

Managing Expectorations

Let's go back a few years; about twenty-five thousand, in fact. A group of Cro-Magnon-types is sitting around a fire, just about ready to figure out how to make images upon a cave wall. These people in southwestern Europe, along with others in places like Africa and Australia, had been making a kind of creative magic by shaping objects into shamanistic forms for about fifteen thousand years. But now they were about to make the conceptual leap of taking their three-dimensional ideas and compressing them onto a flat plane.

We live in a world where we move back and forth effortlessly between two-dimensional symbols and their three-dimensional counterparts, but only because we've been conditioned from a very early age to recognize the nomenclature and the conventions we've devised to interpret a squashed circle as somebody's head, or an ellipse as the chest of a rhinoceros. Try to imagine, however, the kind of abstract thought—the leap of genius, in fact—that must have been required to perform that translation for the first time.

So how did it happen? Did one of the people sitting around the campfire 25,000 BP (before present) suddenly announce, "Ya know, I've been watching those big, woolly bison out on the steppe over the last couple of weeks, and I keep thinking that they move with real elegance and power. Don't you think it would be great if we could capture that dynamic, that grace, in a sweeping gestural line on that wall right there?" Did everyone else nod and say, "Hey, great concept!" Did they form a committee to search out earth pigments and carefully test what

Two Bisons, one of which is cowering. Prehistoric cave painting, Altamira Caves, Spain. Courtesy of Scala/Art Resource, NY.

could be added as a binder to formulate a permanent application?

I don't think so; that's not the road traveled most commonly by human invention. We usually find the really great ideas by accident, and some really bright individual is on hand to recognize the opportunity that has just dropped from the sky, thanks to the magic of serendipity.

It's far more likely that those Cro-Magnon types were sitting around the campfire, munching upon a particularly greasy cut of cave bear haunch. One poor fellow, his mouth still full, reaches to the ground, thinking he's making a grab for a clean stick with which to pick his teeth. Instead, through some wonderful stoke of happenstance, the stick has been resting in a concentrated deposit of what, some twenty-five thousand years later, we call a manganese oxide. He fills his mouth with a fateful combination of pigment and the fat from the bear butt. What's he do when he tastes all of this dirt in his mouth? The same thing you'd do. He leans over and spits onto the rock beside him.

Maybe in the light of the morning sun, he (or she, because genius isn't gender specific) notices that the splat of color is quite vivid and, even more interesting, it's quite stubborn about coming off. Bingo. An early marriage of pigment and binder. Maybe the night before, he was even sloppy enough to spit the mixture over his hand as it rested upon the rock, and the image of his digits have been magically left in reverse, the color filling the space around his fingers. He probably thinks that some astonishing necromancy has happened, catching and keeping some part of his spirit within the image.

Through this scenario, it's not hard to see how the next step is to look for ways to capture the spirits of the magnificent animals that feed the community. It must have seemed like a magical, shamanistic power never before imagined by these people. Painting was born.

This scenario is exactly the same as that created on countless other occasions over the course of human history, with countless other materials, to arrive at countless new and revolutionary opportunities. More often than some of us scientific-method-ites would like to admit, the course of human history is fundamentally changed by someone doing something as accidental as spitting out a mouthful of fat and dirt (or some equally unexpected mixture), and recognizing the breathless potential for a new way of seeing

the world in the expectorated image on the rock at his or her feet.

In the last twenty-five thousand years, the same kind of scenario led to tempera colors, oil colors, acrylic colors, countless new pigments, and who-knows-what else. And the results have been equally revolutionary.

Let's look at how a few key events or issues have shifted the course of artistic (and in some cases cultural) history:

The Cro-Magnon Connection

We've already talked about the imaginary but not-too-far-fetched circumstances under which a cave person or two might have made the original connection that led to permanent two-dimensional images. But there's another question that I simply can't resist: What materials were used by the Cro-Magnons to practice and hone their skills? You don't just decide one day to make an image of a woolly rhino on a cave wall, and then create—on your first try—an image drafted with confidence, surety, and drama. As every one of you reading this book knows, making such an image takes years of practice, observation, and more than a few mistakes. How and upon what did these people do their practice sketching?

The pigments used during pre-history were primarily the red and yellow earths and carbon black, all of which are still in use today, in some form or another. By mixing the pigment with a vehicle of animal fat, and then applying the color with saliva, the Cro-Magnons invented a basic watercolor and the essential elements of painting that would be used for the next twenty-five millennia.

The Invention of Serious Chemistry

We tend to forget that real chemistry isn't all that new. True, the understanding and manipulation of molecular processes have evolved at an exponential rate over the last century, but the transformation of one chemical compound into another was first explored by the Egyptians, Chinese, and Greeks. Over the fifteen to twenty thousand years that it took for more sophisticated cultures to evolve from the Cro-Magnons, painters have had the chance to experiment with a steadily increasing variety of pigments and vehicles.

When talking about the explosion of new materials available to twenty-first century artists, Robert

The Egyptians were among the first to develop a "palette" of colors for painting. This group of historical pigments was sent to Winsor & Newton, in Wealdstone, England, in 1945. The chief chemist at Winsor & Newton, Mr. Shipman, prepared the washes. Courtesy of Winsor & Newton.

Gamblin, of Gamblin Artists Colors, notes that, "Nothing is made just for us." What he means is that many of the really great technological advancements in artists' materials have come as a result of developments in other, more commercially viable, industries. In a following section, we'll take a closer look at what this has meant to our community over the last two hundred years, but it's a safe bet that the trend began a few thousand years ago with the sophisticated economies of the Egyptians and Chinese.

One of the earliest blues used by Egyptian and Chinese painters was indigo, a colorant taken from different plants of the genus *Indigofera*. Its most common use was as a dye for coloring cloth, a commercial application that had obvious value for people who wore clothes (a population that, both then and now, is much larger than the group of people dedicated to making art). Even so, it wasn't long before somebody figured out that the indigo colorant could be ground into a powder and used as a pigment for painting.

Indigo is an early example of how artists' materi-

als have commonly been adapted from products developed for larger, more commercial markets. This isn't to say that we don't come up with our own share of creative innovations (for example, the first paint tube invented by James Rand in 1840, and brought to market by Winsor & Newton in 1842), it's just that we're not ashamed to take advantage of opportunities that come out of other industries.

This is a good place to say that some of the most creative people in the artist materials community aren't the painters or the marketing-types; they're the chemists and technical people, and they often don't get the credit they deserve. Many of the new products that have made such a profound impact upon our community over the last few years are the result of a chemist in a lab wondering, "What if..."

Back to our historical timeline... The Egyptians were making use of gums and waxes for their colors, and the Chinese used glues rendered from animal hides. In the search to widen their coloristic options, both did some pretty great, albeit dangerous, work with pigment chemistry. For example, the Chinese

Cinnabar, the principal ore of mercury, was crushed and ground very early as natural Vermilion. Courtesy of Winsor & Newton.

Vermilion pigment (mercuric sulfide) replaced crushed cinnabar as the dominant red colorant for artists. The process of combining mercury and sulfur was developed very early, probably by the Chinese, and then most likely carried to the west by the Moors. Courtesy of Winsor & Newton.

seem to have been the first to use cinnabar, the raw ore form of mercury, first by grinding it into a red powder, and then by conversion with sulfur into mercuric sulfide, or Vermilion. The pigment was the only brilliant warm red available, and it found its way onto the incised oracle bones of China during the second century B.C. Vermillion was also known to the Greeks and Romans, having been found in Pompeian and Roman walls. Even though manufacturing the pigment can be quite toxic, it continued to be used through the Middle Ages, the Renaissance, and even until recently, when it was replaced by cadmium reds. In the last few years—now that its toxicity has been thoroughly documented—Vermilion has fallen almost entirely from use on a world-wide basis.

In developing asphaltum as an ingredient for mummification, the Egyptians inadvertently created pigments that found their way onto the artist's palette centuries later. (More on that fascinating, and more than a little macabre, pigment in a later section.)

The Artist's Studio

Until the thirteenth and fourteenth centuries in Europe, life for artists progressed fairly steadily, with the introduction of a few new pigments here and there, and the refinement of vehicles made from gums, glues, and waxes. The first major change in the life of the artist came with the evolution of the

Making fine color takes time, care, and more than a bit of muscle. Here, pigment is ground into suspension with a traditional stone muller. Courtesy of Winsor & Newton.

"The Battle of San Romano in 1432," by Paolo Uccello (1397-1475), 1456, egg tempera, done in three panels for the Medici palace. National Gallery, London. Courtesy of Erich Lessing/Art Resource, NY.

studio system. Again, this didn't just happen because a bunch of artist-types said, "Hey let's develop a studio system to gain a bit more status and bring some organization to our trade." As much as many of us like to think that art has always been an exercise in altruistic and aesthetic purity, the making of images has always had (and will always have) a healthy commercial side.

The studio system evolved out of a clear need in the market. The Catholic Church was experiencing a rapid rise in both power and prestige, and there was an equally rapid increase in demand for religious art objects. Political and economic systems were changing as well, resulting in wealthy families that saw real advantages—commercial and political, as well as altruistic—in acting as patrons for the arts. The result was the working studio.

Under this system, young people desiring a trade in art went to work as apprentices with an established artist. The apprentices were responsible for grinding pigment with the appropriate vehicle, preparing the panels and grounds, making brushes, running errands, and sweeping up. More senior apprentices had the privilege of doing some of the preliminary painting work on a project. The artist's job was to work with the patrons, develop images,

and paint.

Pigments were obtained at the local apothecary shop and ground carefully, and with no small measure of sweat, with the chosen vehicle. In a later chapter, we'll detail what makes great paint, but for now, let's just say that making paint isn't like mixing pancake batter. You don't toss a spoonful of pigment into a bowl, pour in a cup of your chosen vehicle, and whip until smooth. The object with making fine color is to coat each and every particle of pigment with an even layer of vehicle. That means grinding and milling for hours, maybe even days, until the color goes into perfect suspension.

And that's not all. Every pigment is different. Some have greater absorption rates with the vehicle, some pigments are made of particles that are heavy and gritty, while others are small and smooth. The specific characteristics of each pigment dictates how much of a given vehicle is needed, as well as how it should be milled. The process of making great color is a skill that has taken me years to appreciate. And the better I've come to understand the process, the greater my awe and appreciation for the people who do it well.

During the Middle Ages and early Renaissance, a variety of vehicles was being used, but the most

common was a tempera made by forming an emulsion with an egg yolk and water. (What's an emulsion, you ask? It's a mixture of substances that don't normally combine through simple mix-and-shake means. Whether through mechanical or chemical means, emulsions have been made for thousands of years, with wax and water, egg and water, and, yes, even oil and water. More on that later.)

For centuries, the term "tempera" was applied to a variety of vehicles (gum tempera, glue tempera, and egg tempera). Beginning, however, in the middle Renaissance, with the development of oils as a vehicle, tempera came to refer almost exclusively to the emulsion made with egg.

A quick comparison of paintings created during the early Renaissance with egg tempera and those employed later with oil serve as a lovely example of how the character and quality of the vehicle can alter the course of image making. Both mediums have their ups and down in terms of preparation, use, and clean-up. Tempera requires frequent grinding of color, while oils required those less-than-pleasant solvents (remember there was no odorless mineral spirit available from the corner colourman).

But the real differences show up on the surface of the painting. Tempera leaves a relatively flat, uniform tonality. The colors dry very rapidly, allowing little time for surface blending. While the pattern and rhythm in The Battle of San Romano (on page 15) make for an undeniably wonderful painting, the work also clearly illustrates how the very nature of tempera leads to an image of minimal depth and flat tonality.

Oils, on the other hand, could be adapted to create different finishes. The handling of oils was almost infinitely variable, allowing for rounder, fuller modeling. They afforded the painter the opportunity to take full advantage of the individual pigments' character, applying color in varying degrees of opacity and transparency. Glazing was possible, and astonishing new depth and richness was the result. Looking at Jan van Eyck's The Arnolfini Wedding, painted in 1434 and regarded as one of the earliest examples of oil as a medium, the differences come into stark relief. The exquisite modeling of the figures, the playful rendering of the image in the mirror, and the sublime play of light throughout the space—all were possible only because of the oil vehicle.

(left) "The Arnolfini Wedding," by Jan van Eyck (c. 1390-1441), 1434, oil (with some tempera) on panel. National Gallery, London. Courtesy of Erich Lessing/Art Resource, NY.

It's safe to say that had oil not been developed as a vehicle for color, the entire course of art history would have been different. Not only would there have been no Arnolfini portrait, we wouldn't be marveling at the transcendental rendering of light by Vermeer, we wouldn't have the drama of Rembrandt, or the shimmering dynamics of Monet.

The transition by the Renaissance painting community from tempera to oil is one of the most illuminating moments in art history, illustrating how the fundamental character of the materials makes a profound difference in the character of the finished work. And that's the best argument for two premises that you'll read time and time again in this volume:

1. Know your materials. The better you understand what your tools can and can't do, the more effectively you'll be able to use them with success. Never doubt that your understanding of the materials will show up in the quality of your work.

2. Buy the best quality materials you can afford. There are very real reasons that some products cost more than others (we'll outline them all in later chapters). And, as above, never doubt that the quality of those materials will show up in the quality of your work.

The Trade of the Colourman

In the middle part of the seventeenth century, a new business evolved in Europe: the colourman. Again, the primary market for milling and selling paint was in larger arenas than the artist's trade, and

The corner colourman shop is a relatively new development for artists. Above is the shop of Winsor & Newton, as founded at 38 Rathbone Place, London, in 1832.

there were more than a few colourmen keeping busy by selling colour for house painting, or scene painting for the theater. But, there was enough of a market in supplying professional artists, not to mention the beginnings of an amateur movement in painting, that there were a few colourmen who offered products for the artistic-type. Colours, brushes, and panels could be purchased off the shelf.

Global trade had become more fluid and far-reaching, bringing more new pigments to market. Perhaps because of these expanded trade routes and resources, a new colour showed up at the end of the sixteenth century, a brown called "mummy." Here's where the aforementioned work of the Egyptians arrived on European palettes. There's not much of a historical record of the color (perhaps out of the justifiable embarrassment on the part of those who obtained the raw materials), and it's hard to know if the artists who made use of the color understood its

One of the more unusual pigments ever used was that made of ground Egyptian mummies. Its use was, thankfully, short-lived. Courtesy of Winsor & Newton.

Genuine Indian yellow pigment. Today, the color named Indian yellow is usually made from a synthetic pigment. Its original incarnation was precipitated from the urine of Indian cattle, which fed upon mango leaves. Courtesy of Winsor & Newton.

true origin. It's easy to see how someone might view the name as just a handy trade identifier: "Surely this can't be made from real mummies," would be my initial thought. "Can it?"

It could and it was. Asphaltum used during the mummification process gave the color a specific character. It also wasn't long before someone figured out that using straight asphaltum as a pigment gave the same result, not to mention the variety of bituminous earth pigments that were available. Thankfully, the use of mummy brown was short-lived, so to speak.

While mummy brown is a clear example of how pigments have come from strange sources, here's one that clearly falls in the category of "what could possibly have made someone think this up?" A book published in 1805, entitled *Essay on Light and Shade*, by Gartside, includes an early mention of a color imported from India called Indian yellow. The color was reasonably resistant to fading, used primarily in watercolors, and was considered to be a beautiful shade, particularly well-suited for rendering landscapes. It was also known by the poetic name of Indian puree.

Indian yellow was made from the urine of cattle at Monghyr in Bengal, specifically those animals that were fed a steady diet of mango leaves. The urine was heated to precipitate a yellow substance that was dried and then pressed into lumps the size of a small apple.

I can imagine the Cro-Magnon happy accident that led to the invention of painting. I'm at a loss, however, to come up with an imagined scenario that led to the invention of Indian puree.

The Motor Car

Huh? What does the automobile have to do with the history of art materials? Bear with me.

Wrap up all of the history that's been outlined over these last pages, and you can see that, up until about two hundred years ago, the only colors available to artist-types were difficult to obtain, uneven in quality, and painfully limited in range and hue. The reds and oranges were poisonous (sometimes to a deadly degree), and the blues were terribly difficult to make and outrageously expensive. The only colors available with much consistency were earth colors, the natural iron oxides that could be dug from the earth in a variety of subdued shades of browns, reds, and yellows.

Pigment samples in a sales case used in the 1880s. Courtesy of Winsor & Newton.

While a lake pigment may still exhibit some dye-like characteristics, through staining and bleeding, it will remain in stable suspension when milled into color.)

Over the following two-and-a-half centuries, the synthetic process that created Prussian blue would turn the trickle of new pigments and products into a torrent. From Prussian blue to the present, things have happened all in a rush.

In 1828, J.B. Guimet won a 6,000 franc prize for being the first to discover a method of making an artificial ultramarine blue that could be brought to market for no more than 300 francs per kilogram. Why the prize and why the stipulation on market cost? Because, before Guimet's method, ultramarine was made only from the finest lapis lazuli, a stunning blue stone found in various parts of the globe. The finest lapis comes, however, from the Kokcha Valley in what is present-day Afghanistan. Natural ultramarine had been in use for centuries before Guimet's new method of making it artificially, but only at extreme expense. As a result of Guimet's outstanding chemistry, we now have the pleasure of painting with

It's during the eighteenth century that we can see the first trickle of new, artificially prepared products for artists. Prussian blue was the first artificially synthesized color, developed by a colour maker named Diesbach sometime around 1705. Once again, the invention was an accident.

It seems that, during the process of preparing a Florentine lake color, Diesbach made inadvertent use of some potash that had been contaminated with a distilled animal oil. Instead of getting an intense red lake, he got something much paler. When he tried to adjust the color further, it turned purple and then deep blue. Prussian blue, in fact; a pigment that was a truly new, never-before-made-by-nature compound.

(Note: Just for purposes of clarity, a "lake" color is made when a dye is chemically "adjusted" to work like a pigment. Remember that dyes bleed, and pigments remain in suspension within the paint vehicle. A dye can be made to think it's a pigment—and to act like one, as well—when it's attached or precipitated onto an inert base, like aluminum hydrate.

Lapis stone from Afghanistan and natural ultramarine pigment. Perhaps no pigment has been written about more, or described with more poetry, than natural ultramarine ground from pure lapis lazuli. Courtesy of Winsor & Newton.

Frontispiece, *Pinnock's Catechism of the Practice of Painting in Oils*, 1823. Courtesy of Winsor & Newton.

a compound that has a molecular structure virtually identical to that of the original lapis.

While researching this book, I had the extraordinary opportunity to review some of the archived historical materials at Winsor & Newton in Wealdstone, England. Sitting at a large wooden table, I stared at a selection of painting texts and formulation notebooks dating back to 1756, twenty years before the upstart American colonists declared their independence, about forty years before the invention of making paper upon a machine rather than exclusively by hand, and on the cusp of the Industrial Revolution, when new colors would bring a myriad of fresh options to the painter's palette. Wearing cotton gloves, I turned the pages with great care, listening to the soft whispers of brittle paper and marveling at the smells that came from the open books, odors that come only with great age.

There was a small pocket text entitled *Pinnock's Catechism of the Practice of Painting in Oils*, published by G & WB Whittaker in 1823. The text was written in a question and answer format, and my eye fell upon one answer to a query about lapis ultramarine. "Ultra-marine is the finest blue in the world and never glares," read the text. "It is used in the pearly hues of the flesh and azure tints of the sky, which no other colour will reach." Oh man, as a writer, how do you top "pearly hues" and "azure tints"? If that's not the best description for the magic to be found in color, I don't know what is.

The same kind of chemistry that brought low-cost ultramarine to market in 1828 happens today, as well. As we barrel into the new millennium, the old sources of iron oxides and earth pigments that made the very finest, brightest, and most transparent siennas and umbers are becoming increasingly difficult to obtain. But thanks to the wonders of modern chemistry, color manufacturers can make use of a range of synthetic iron oxides that are highly comparable to the original pigments, both in chemical structure and in performance.

By the early portions of nineteenth century, chemistry had evolved to a point where metals like cadmium, cobalt, or manganese could be combined chemically with other compounds. The results were products, like cadmium sulfide (which could be "adjusted" by adding varying degrees of selenium to make oranges and reds), that were highly stable, far

Until the development of the tube for storing color, paints were often kept in bound pig bladders. Courtesy of Winsor & Newton.

less prone to fading, and that could be ground into a suspension within a vehicle like linseed oil for oil paint.

All of a sudden, there was a whole galaxy of stable and dependable pigments available, and the Impressionists took full advantage of new colors like cerulean blue (1860), alizarin (1868), and aureolin (1889), changing our perception of the world in the process. Even more pigments became available around the turn of the century (Hansa yellow in 1899, cadmium red around 1910), and the flowering of color that had come with the Impressionists became an explosion. The exhilarating, brazen color palette of painters like Gauguin and Kandinsky made a joyful painterly noise, the likes of which had never before been seen. And all because of new pigment chemistry.

There were other advancements that came with the Industrial Revolution, as well. Until the middle of the nineteenth century, paint was carried about in things like less-than-convenient pig bladders. Then, in 1842, Winsor & Newton bought the patent for a stoppered metal tube from its inventor, a painter named James Goffe Rand. Winsor & Newton

replaced the stopper with a screw cap, and paint was brought to market for the first time in a simple, easy-to-dispense package. How much did the paint tube contribute to the blossoming of the Impressionist movement? It's impossible to say, but there's no question that on-site, "alla prima" painting became much easier with the advent of a simple means of carrying color.

As should be painfully clear by now, all of these scientific and color-chemical-types weren't working their behinds off in the lab because somebody thought there was a fortune to be made in selling artists' paints. Our community is deeply dependent upon—and indebted to—a host of other industries. Robert Gamblin notes that, "Today, the biggest use of cadmium colors is for coloring plastic, and the biggest use for the manganese colors is for aluminum siding." In short, without the plastics industry, and without people needing aluminum siding on their homes, there might well be no cadmium red or cerulean blue artists' colors.

Not too far into the twentieth century, our community received a gift from the plastics industry. In the 1940s, a few free-thinking pioneers started playing

The availability of new colors, along with convenient packaging in tubes, allowed painters to develop images in ways never before possible. "The Artist's Garden At Giverny," by Claude Monet (1840-1926), 1900. Courtesy of Giraudon/Art Resource, NY.

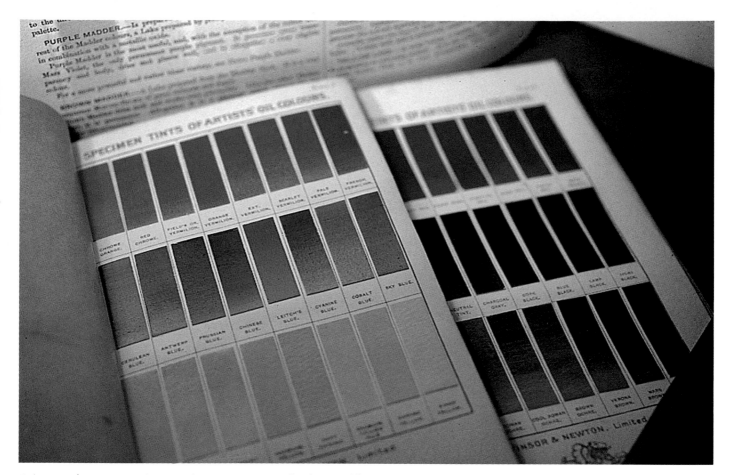

Selection of specimen color tints, showing a mixture of colors used for centuries, alongside new pigments that changed how artists used color, and, in the process, altered our view of the world. 1870–90. Courtesy of Winsor & Newton.

Pioneers with a new medium. The use of acrylic polymer as a vehicle for pigment was first explored by Lenny Bocour and Sam Golden in the 1940s and '50s. Courtesy of Golden Artist Color.

with acrylic polymer for use as a vehicle with pigment. The results of experiments by people like Lenny Bocour and Sam Golden was a medium that, now at the turn of the twenty-first century, outsells traditional oils and watercolors. Just like when oils supplanted tempera in the fifteenth century, new applications and techniques became possible because of the new medium. It's hard to imagine Helen Frankenthaler, Morris Louis, or David Hockney producing their characteristic work without the specific qualities—once again, quite different than the character of oils or of watercolor—that come only with acrylic colors.

As it became clear to early twentieth-century marketing gurus that making things in different colors meant better sales of just about anything, it also became clear that new sources for color would be needed, as well. There was also the element of cost that comes with, as noted by Robert Gamblin, "heading to Zaire to dig up half the country for a load of cadmium or cobalt. There are a lot of reasons for the (color chemistry) industry to look for new solutions in our own backyard. Hence the experimentation with organic carbon compounds."

In the early nineteenth century, German chemists began to experiment with making pigment from carbon compounds. By then, it had been determined

"Small's Paradise," by Helen Frankenthaler (b. 1928), 1964, acrylic on canvas, 8' 4" x 7' 9-5/8". Courtesy of the National Museum of American Art, Smithsonian Institute, Washington, DC (Gift of George I. Erion)/Art Resource, NY. © 2000 Helen Frankenthaler. Acrylics are a different animal altogether. They offer an astonishing range of viscosity, from high fluidity to sculptural, high-peak impasto. Helen Frankenthaler, along with artists like Morris Louis and Barnett Newman, were among the first to take advantage of the new medium's capabilities.

that carbon, oxygen, hydrogen, and nitrogen can be twisted, broken apart, braided, tied, and jammed together to create new things that hadn't before seen the light of day.

The Germans came up with an arylide compound, a brand-spanking new yellow, that they christened "Hansa" yellow. It was soon found that Hansa yellow and its brethren (compounds like naphthols, the quinacridones, and the phthalocyanines) could be synthesized as dyes (a compound that goes into solution within its solvent or vehicle, and that bleeds into surrounding materials like crazy), or as pigments (a compound that remains a discrete particle, and can be ground into a suspension within a vehicle).

Bingo! A whole new colorful world opened to industrial designers, clothing manufacturers, printers, and everyone on the planet who wanted to add color to their product.

Especially those guys making cars.

Emma Pearce puts it quite plainly: "You've got to say, thank goodness for the motor car. It's really the car finish industry that drives new colours to the level of permanence that we require in the art materials industry."

To make a long story short, the evolution of synthetic, organic pigments continued at a steady pace into the 1960s. Then things really got rolling.

Early in the 1990s, Winsor & Newton began the process of reformulating all of its artist ranges. Why? "Because, for most of the twentieth century," says Pearce, "there were one or two new colours introduced, here and there. But, by the time we got to the late '80s, there was an amazing new generation of pigments available. And the new pigments offered the greatest degree of lightfastness, and the most balanced spectrum, that anyone had ever seen. We felt just that it (reformulating the ranges) was the right thing to do."

There were perinones and pyrroles and benzimidazolone, to name just a few. Naphthols, which had been around for decades, have been revisited to create new, more lightfast hues. And, aside from the tortuous, tongue-tangling names, each one of them represents fabulous, new opportunities for artists.

I made the point early on that twenty-first century artists' materials are better than anything ever before produced. Here are a few reasons why that statement applies to colors:

Quinacridone red is just one of the burgeoning family of synthetically derived pigments. The most recent generation of synthetic organic colors now rivals traditional pigments in lightfastness and boosts the options available to artists to levels never before imagined. Courtesy of Winsor & Newton.

Today's Colors Mix With Greater Consistency

Most fine art manufacturers are talking about their colors as being in three tribes: the earths, the inorganics, and the organics.

The earths are colors that are dug directly from the ground (like the siennas or the umbers), or are synthesized (like the iron oxides). Members of the inorganic tribe include all of the colors thought of as traditional, like cadmium and cobalt.

As has been known for a few generations now, the earths and inorganics offer lightfastness that ranges from good to last-till-the-end-of-time. (Note: Check the manufacturer ratings listed on tubes. Makers of fine color have been proven to be quite conscientious in identifying the lightfast qualities of their colors.) And both tribes tend to be great for mixing the colors that come with painting in natural light.

Across the available range of organic pigments, lightfastness has seen a big jump, now being (in most cases) at least as secure as most inorganic pigments. And the selection has increased dramatically, making for a spectrum that has greater "balance," and can be mixed with greater "cleanliness," purity, and control than ever before.

The Selection Is Intoxicating, Not to Mention the Creative Opportunities

"The pinks and violets available now," says Pearce, "are beyond the wildest dreams of past painters. To have those sorts of magentas and violets that are permanent in flower painting is just unbelievable!"

It's not just floral painters that have new opportunities at hand. Since their introduction, the organics

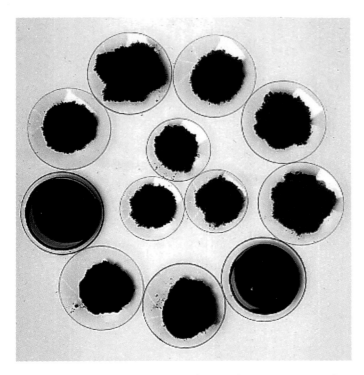

It's not just the new pigments made from synthetic sources, it's also the sheer numbers that have become available. Here are twelve different phthalocyanine blue pigments, a color with tinting strength too strong to be milled into color by itself. Phthalo blue always requires some form of extender to allow mixing and tinting that compares to other colors on the artist's palette. Courtesy of Winsor & Newton.

have been saddled with a perception of being poor step-children to the "real" colors, those towering paragons of coloristic virtue, the cadmiums and cobalts. Well, it's time for that perception to go away. Or, as Gamblin says, "Hansa yellow is not a cadmium wannabe!"

The organic colors have always been recognized as being superior to inorganic colors when painting bright, high-key images. Over the last few years, they've begun to gain increased acceptance as colors for glazing (their natural transparency offers a tremendous advantage), and as a complement, or a "supercharger," to the inorganic palette. "Something that grays down quickly, like a viridian," notes Gamblin, "where you wanted something a little more vibrant, can be boosted with phthalo green or a phthalo green yellow shade. You get something with the original depth of the viridian, but not nearly so muted. You can control the intensity of the color by combining the two together."

In some cases, new pigments have even become a welcome replacement for original colors. Now that the sources for some great natural earth pigments (the siennas and umbers with which Rembrandt set

more than a few aesthetic standards) are diminishing, "transparent earth" synthetic substitutes offer a highly satisfactory alternative.

If you think that pigment chemistry has been a rodeo over the last few decades, wait until you see what's coming out of the chute over the next few years. Golden Artist Colors has introduced a line of acrylic colors called "Panspectra™," a range that's sure to raise eyebrows and standards. Panspectra is made from a multi-layer pigment that reflects different hues, depending upon the viewing angle. For example, the cyan-purple product "flips" from cyan to green to purple to red as you move around the image. "There are more choices available than ever before for the manufacturer," says Anthony Sorosky, Director of Marketing for Golden Artist Colors, "and that means more choices for artists."

The Vehicle Has Evolved to Unsurpassed Levels of Stability

This one's pretty simple. The technology and chemistry used for processing, creating, and stabilizing the vehicles used in making artists' color is better than ever before. That, and the processes used in making the materials, has become far more environmentally friendly.

The Apple and My Mistake

My apprenticeship in the art products community was spent in art materials stores. I had the chance to research and answer questions from thousands of artists and creative-types. I had the opportunity to establish relationships with artists and manufacturers that have blossomed over the last twenty years into deep friendships.

The retail store was also where I made some of my most memorable mistakes. The one that I remember most vividly came when I was asked by a business partner what I thought about the long-term impact of a new little something on the market: a funny-looking, ochre-gray box called the Macintosh. The year was 1986.

I said something like, "Oh, it's interesting, for sure. And it may well find a place on designer's desks for some applications. But it's hard to see how the problems with color output will ever be solved, so I don't think it will ever fully replace all the products behind our graphic arts counter."

Ha! Talk about head-in-the-sand syndrome and self-deception! After a few years, the error of that

Golden Panspectra™ is one of the latest pigments to reach the market. Panspectra is a multi-layered pigment that reflects different hues, depending upon viewing angle. Courtesy of Golden Artist Colors.

statement became blatantly clear, and I swore that I'd never again ignore or dismiss developing technologies and ideas. And it's now clear that any discussion of historical revolutions in the use of color has to include electronic media.

Chapter 6 details some of the issues and information that will be helpful to artists making use of this astonishing, and rapidly evolving, new medium. Right now it's enough to say that the computer is loaded with every bit as much creative magic as a brush or a palette full of paint. And here's a newsflash for anyone who says that the computer will never occupy a place in the fine artist's studio: there were more than a few of us who made the mistake of dissing the Mac once; we shouldn't do it again.

Whether for a Cro-Magnon shaman, a calligrapher in China, a color chemist, a dedicated painter, an artist on the Macintosh, or my four-year-old daughter with her crayons and day-lily sticks, there is deep and powerful magic in color. And no matter how the mediums, the chemistry, and the formats change, that magic has always been there, and I'm sure that it always will.

A Duck Is a Duck Is a Duck

"We are required to call a duck by a proper duck's name," observes Robert Gamblin with a dry tone in his voice.

The ASTM committee devoted to artists' materials is requiring accuracy in label names. That's a good thing. But there's no question that the polysyllabic names first developed by German chemists in the early twentieth century have proven to be the biggest barrier to market acceptance of organic colors. There's romance and history in cadmium, cobalt, cerulean, sienna, and umber, while it's hard to fall in love with something called quinacridone or dioxazine or, heaven forbid, benzimidazolone.

"It may be that the benzimidazolones, as a group of colors, are better than the arylide or diarylide colors. But I despair of bringing them to market because of the tremendous difficulty (of gaining name acceptance)," says Gamblin.

Winsor & Newton recently took a courageous leap by bringing benzimidazolone orange and maroon to market in its range of Finity Artists' Acrylics. When asked about how benzimidazolone orange is faring on the open market, and the obligation to label with correct pigment names, Emma Pearce responds by saying, "Well, put it this way. Winsor blue didn't become an accepted part of the palette until the beginning of the '80s, and it had been out forty years."

So why do it? Pearce adds, "You don't launch twenty or thirty new colours on the idea that you're going to sell vast quantities from the very beginning. And if you were only going for the amateur market, then calling things by a craft name would sell you more colours. You know, 'mid-green one' or 'mid-green two' are going to sell you more than colors with names they can't even say. But, from our point of view, it's a long-term investment. And for dedicated artists, it's the right thing to do."

What do we do with benzimidazolone? "Maybe we should just call it 'Betsy,'" suggests Gamblin with a chuckle.

(above) In some respects, benzimidazolone is the poster child for modern pigments: a color of remarkable purity and lightfastness, but saddled with a tongue-twister name. Courtesy of Winsor & Newton.

Chapter 2
Color My World:
The Emotional Impact of Color

Color mixing triads, comparing two different ranges of artists' color. Courtesy of Winsor & Newton.

The central question for me, as I began this chapter, was whether or not to include a photo of myself in a pink tutu.

Let's back up. Over the past few years, I've had some success conducting a workshop that includes a discussion of the impact of color for artists, craftspeople, retail merchandisers, and other interested creative-types. The crux of the presentation is that, at a basic, visceral level, color carries emotional weight. Every one of us responds to color with some degree of emotion, sometimes quite strongly.

The presentation begins with a list of the primary, secondary, and a few tertiary colors projected upon a screen. Next to the name of each color are a few words describing the emotional response most commonly associated with that color. But this is a visual audience, right? A list with a few associated descriptors isn't going to be enough. So, after the audience has had a few moments to digest the list, I make use of a few selected props to illustrate the rich emotional character that we all ascribe, in various degrees, to certain colors. Here's how the list (and the use of props) progresses:

• **Red: aggressive, passionate, strong**
(The author unbuttons his shirt to expose a red Superman "S" upon his T-shirt.)
• **Orange: fun, cheerful, warm, exuberant**
(The author pulls a sheet of flash paper and a match from his pocket, sending a burst of orange flame over the heads of those lucky few in the first couple of rows.)

- **Yellow: positive, sunshine**
(The author lifts a bright yellow yo-yo from the bag of props upon the front table. Those who survived the orange burst of flame get to play with the new toy.)
- **Green: tranquil, healthy, fresh**
(The author dons a green Hawaiian lei.)
- **Blue: authoritative, dignified, secure**
(The author pulls a doll from the bag. In 1996, the doll was republican presidential candidate Bob Dole. In 1998, it was special prosecutor Kenneth Starr. The author is unable to predict who'll be next.)
- **Purple: sophisticated, expensive, royal**
(The author ties a lush, purple robe about his shoulders.)
- **Brown: utilitarian, earthy, subtly rich**
(A small, brown Winnie-the-Pooh doll is thrown to the audience.)
- **Gray: somber, authoritative, practical, corporate**
(A gray toy brain is handed to someone in the front row. "Hang on to that, please," says the author. "I don't want to lose my mind.")
- **Black: serious, distinctive, bold, classic**
(The author dons a black, elasticized bow tie.)
- **White: pure, truthful, refined**
(With apologies to Catholics in the audience [and in the readership], the author places a high, white cardinal's miter upon his head.)
- **Pink: feminine, innocent, soft, healthy**
(With no small amount of grunting and twisting, the author pulls a [painfully] tight pink tutu about his waist.)

(Thanks to the Color Marketing Group for this illuminative list.)

Where does the visceral response to color originate? Much of it clearly comes from cultural reinforcement; repeated exposure to Superman with that scarlet "S" upon his chest ensures that red is unavoidably associated with super-virility. Purple has long been associated with royalty, at least as far back as the Greeks, when the color secreting cyst of as many as twelve thousand whelks (a kind of mollusk in the Mediterranean) were squeezed to produce a gram or two of Tyrian purple colorant for imperial robes.

There's reason to believe that the response goes back much further than those two examples. It doesn't take a huge leap to deduce that the red response probably originated with the sight of the blood of animals killed during hunts by the same Cro-Magnon

Color computer, used for measuring the colometric properties of pigments. Courtesy of Winsor & Newton.

types who also invented painting.

The point to the color-and-prop demonstration outlined above—and to this discussion, as well—is to make it very clear that color carries some serious emotional baggage. The props used during my lecture entertain and, more important, help people clearly associate and then remember the typical response to specific colors. But for artists, painters, and anyone really serious about color, we need to take this discussion at least a step or two further. We need to look at how pigments and different mediums can help in exploring the full range of expressive relationships among colors.

The "In-between" of Color

With spectrophotometric measurement, we can identify where a specific hue of red (or blue or green or whatever) falls within a color spectrum. We can measure all of the physical, optical, and spectral properties of a particular color within an inch of its visual, infrared, and ultraviolet life. But identifying the physical properties of a color doesn't make someone a painter, any more than knowing that the tone "A" on the piano is in tune at 440 vibrations per second makes someone capable of composing a symphony.

Art is much more than the mechanical application

Josef Albers, book cover exercise (plate IV-1 in the unabridged version, 1963, Yale University Press). Courtesy of Yale University Press.

above. Look at the image and try to determine if the two central, ochre squares of color are different. Clearly, the one above the blue and yellow center bars is a lighter color. Isn't it? And there's no question that the lower square is the darker of the two. Right?

In fact, the two squares are identical. We perceive them differently, however, because of the relationships that each has with adjacent colors and those that serve as grounds. And the implications of this illustration, along with Albers' remark about the "in-between of the tones," become quite clear. A mature understanding of color requires far more than a basic grasp of the tonal and spectral characteristics (not to mention the emotional associations) that come with individual hues. Dynamic, expressive color comes, first and foremost, out of relationships.

This book isn't really about how to develop your own unique color vocabulary; for that, there are much better teachers and resources (I can't think of a better place to start than with Josef Albers). Rather, it's about how the characteristics of the materials, the pigments, and the vehicles, will enhance your developing color sensibilities. The essential nature of the pigments—their mixing qualities, their natural opacity or transparency, and a host of other characteristics—will have a profound effect upon your ability to cultivate an expressive color vocabulary.

To see how these physical attributes contribute to expressive color, let's undertake...

...A Study in Red

Red isn't just "aggressive, passionate, and strong," as outlined in the earlier (and admittedly oversimplified) list of common responses to color. Depending upon its use within an image, and the characteristics of the pigment chosen, red can convey an incredibly wide range of emotion. Let's take a look at a half-dozen paintings, all of which include red in a central role. We'll look at how the color defines or amplifies the expressive content within the image, and then we'll identify how the physical properties of the pigment and/or vehicle make the color do its job. Before we launch into this exercise, I should mention that, even though this study focuses upon red, it could just as easily be done in blue or purple or yellow.

of line, shape, form, texture, and color. Creative expression arises out of the relationships among those elements, rather than the elements themselves. Using music as a metaphor for the visual arts, master colorist and teacher Josef Albers said it brilliantly in his book *Interaction of Color* (1963, Yale University Press) when he wrote: "...music depends upon the recognition of the in-between of the tones, of their placing and of their spacing."

The principle is true in virtually any discipline. In music, visual art, language and literature, chemistry, physics, and business, the heart of the matter is not in the things themselves, but in the relationships, the "in-between," of the things. And it's ever-so-true when learning about color.

The exercises in Albers' book are among those most commonly used in helping artists develop a unique, personal vocabulary of color. The importance of color relationships (rather than the individual colors, themselves) is easily seen in the illustration

"Abstract Composition," by Helen Frankenthaler (b. 1928), watercolor on paper. Courtesy of Victoria & Albert Museum, London/Art Resource, NY. © 2000 Helen Frankenthaler.

From transparent to opaque, staining to granulating, this image makes wonderful use of a wide array of pigment qualities. The piece also shows off some of the dynamic, calligraphic qualities that come only with highly fluid color. Frankenthaler has created a remarkable tonal contrast between the two reds. The strong, fiery red dominates the bottom (presumably a cadmium) and is contrasted against the cool, blue-bias red (a quinacridone or mixed crimson?) in the center of the green square. Note the bleeding and staining of cool red in the center into the warm ground below and above. Everything has added depth and drama by virtue of the surrounding, complementary green field. Would this image have the strength or dynamic punch if two blues were substituted for the reds? Not a chance.

"Girl with the Red Hat," by Johannes Vermeer, 1665–66, oil on panel. Photograph Board of Trustees, National Gallery of Art, Washington. Andrew W. Mellon Collection.

Vermilion is used for the fur trim on the hat, leaving the girl's face in shadow, while the green tones in shadow add complementary contrast and drama. The color and contrast heighten the girl's mystery and the sense of immediacy in her glance from across a room. Last but not least is the reflection of Vermilion upon her moistened lips. Whew! It's the unique dynamic clarity of Vermilion that carries the undercurrent of passion in this painting.

"Harmony in Red" (The Tablecloth), by Henri Matisse (1869-1954), 1908, oil on canvas. Succession H. Matisse, Paris/ARS, NY. Hermitage, St. Petersburg, Russia. Courtesy of Scala/Art Resource, NY.

With the woman seated in the midst of a domestic scene, this image isn't so much one of virility or passion, as it is of powerful, energetic space. All of the figures and shapes are full of dynamic animation, moving around and through the robust red ground. This is red as pure, unadulterated exuberance. Notice how the tame, natural vista through the window brings some balance to the puissant interior.

In this image, Matisse has made optimal use of the individual qualities that make cadmium colors unique: deep, rich tonality and superb opacity.

"Putney winter heart, 1971–72," by Jim Dine (b. 1935), assemblage. Musee National d'Art Moderne, Centre Georges Pompidou, Paris. Courtesy of Giraudon/Art Resource, NY.

Look at the difference in the reds used on the interior of the heart compared to those on the outer perimeter. All of the colors have been used to create a back-and-forth, push-pull in and about the form. The bold, warm reds in the interior have been set against a cool, blue-bias red (lower left, outside of the heart), a scratchy, fragmented stroke of red (on the right), and a weak, chalky pink at top left. The different reds set up the space and the depth for a fascinating image of a conflicted, passionate, and very complicated heart.

"Nave Na Mahana" (Tahitian Repast), by Paul Gauguin (1848-1903), 1891. Musee des Beaux-Arts, Lyon, France. Courtesy of Giraudon/Art Resource, NY.

Here, a remarkable range of reds has been used to bring depth, richness, and unity to the painting. There are reds that are fiery and passionate, reds that are cool and distant, and some that are warm and comfortable. Red in different temperatures and biases is used to establish the character and space for each figure within the image. In one case, the red is used to heighten a sense of longing. In another, a sense of introspection. In yet another, there is isolation and loneliness. The entire painting is suffused with virtuoso use of red in different hues, tones, and tints.

If red were part of a symphonic orchestra, it would be the brass family. And within that group, there are the warm reds of the French horn, the blaring bright cadmiums of the trumpet, along with the deep earth reds of the trombone and baritone horn. Just like in orchestration, there is timbre and shading within color.

Looking at the previous collection of images, it becomes self-evident why a color chart of artists' quality paints—whether in oil, acrylic, or watercolor—includes as many as ten or twelve different reds. The same is true of blues, greens, violets, and all of the other colors available now, at the turn of the twenty-first century. The wide array of available hues—all differing in transparency, warmth, and pitch—represent a truly infinite range of opportunities to explore the relationships that are possible within your images.

The first two chapters of this book have been written to give you some sense of historical background and creative context. From here forward, the rest of the book is about the tools, and how you can use them to your best—and most expressive—advantage.

Oh yes. About the tutu. I simply couldn't put my wife and children in the position of defending a published photograph of me decked out in a Superman T-shirt, a cardinal's miter, and a tutu. So, this photo will simply have to serve. Use your imagination.

Chapter 3
Film Critics: Making Great Color and Making It Stick

Pay attention and you start to notice it everywhere. More precisely, you start to notice its *disappearance* everywhere. In the fine art world, you see it in museums: the surface cracking on paintings created with oil colors, and the yellowing or discoloration of images. Even more dramatic, you notice the flaking and obvious physical degeneration of work done by artists as recently as a few decades ago. Those frenetic, breathtaking paintings by Jackson Pollack are going to be a challenge for conservators to keep in recognizable shape for more than another generation or two.

We lose color in other places, too; places that— even though they may not carry great aesthetic weight in the larger world—occupy spaces of deep meaning in the lives of an individual or two or three. One recent evening, with my daughter and son play-

Scoops used for pigment. Courtesy of Winsor & Newton.

ing "daddy playground," clambering over my legs and shoulders as I sat upon the floor, I looked up at a framed image on the wall and felt a twinge of sadness. Inside the frame were the handprints of my daughter Jordan, done when she was two by a preschool teacher, in what had once been bright red paint. It's one of those images that gives daily comfort and pleasure, even if— after being hung upon the wall with pride and ceremony—it now registers most often only on the periphery and in passing.

The last time I'd taken full note of the handprints, they'd been markedly different, the digits spread wide and in rich, dynamic color. Now, in the space of a few short months, the color had gone flat and pale. "How much more will the image fade in the next year, and the year after that?" I thought.

Okay, so maybe the fading of my children's handprints isn't a loss that registers on a worldwide scale. But it registers in my heart.

(Note from the author as a dad rather than as an art materials writer: Is there an opportunity here? A chance for a manufacturer to introduce a line of non-toxic color with lightfast pigment in a stable vehicle, expressly for the purpose of ensuring that handprints and keepsakes remain intact for more than a year or two? Call it "memory color," add some descriptive copy, and every mom, dad, grandmom, and grandad on the planet would be happy to pay the extra cost for a stable image.)

A few paintings become critically unstable because of poorly made color. Far greater numbers become unstable because the paint was incorrectly applied. Pollack's paintings are disintegrating because he chose to use house paint, color that's formulated to last but a decade or so. Keepsakes of childhood fade because it's just accepted that we opt for inexpensive color with youngsters, presuming that there's no need to invest in the good stuff. Sometimes that's true. Often it's not. And often the good stuff isn't chosen because the user, whether a dedicated artist or a well-meaning hand-printer, simply doesn't know what makes the good stuff good. That's what this chapter is about:

Step-by-step, How Fine Color is Made

Let's pretend that we're pigment. (Bear with me. I simply can't resist these kinds of little exercises.) And let's look at the process that we would undergo if we were to be transformed from raw material into really great artists' color. First…

…We have to get picked. I always hated this part in school, this waiting to be picked to play on the team. But the simple fact is that, if we're a really fine example of all of the qualities that characterize good pigment, we're going to be picked right away, while those poor sods that don't quite measure up have to hang in line for a while. Here are some of the criteria that are going to be used in selection:

• **Are we clean and pure?** Obviously, pigment that is laden with unwanted flotsam and jetsam isn't going to make the team. Any impurities are going to show up in the final product, altering the color's hue and chroma (brightness).

• **Are we a fine example of our true character?** If we're a cadmium, are we bright, dense, and opaque, like we're supposed to be? If

we're an iron oxide, do we have deep, rich hue and natural transparency? If we're a phthalocyanine, do we glow like stained glass? Every pigment either matches or misses some ideal characteristics that have been developed and accepted over the course of decades, centuries, and even millennia. And the best pigment embodies those ideals as closely as possible.

At times, this issue of true pigment character gets muddy. For example, at the time of this writing, the really great sienna earths are getting more and more difficult to obtain; those that are so vibrant in tone and are beautifully transparent, the ones Rembrandt and Vermeer used in those breathtaking interiors. Those earth pigments are (or were) transparent because of little "prisms" of aluminum silicate that were in the mix. Lesser quality earth pigments don't have that jewel-like transparency.

As the great-quality earth pigment has disap-peared, a synthetic iron oxide has become available (thanks, in fact, to the auto industry) that is compara-ble in rich hue and has the physical structure (like stained glass) to offer lovely transparency. Manufacturers that stick with the old earth pigments won't have either of those qualities.

Things get even more complicated. The American Society for Testing and Materials (ASTM) subcommit-tee on art materials has created a standard (D-4302), encouraging manufacturers to use label names that reflect the specific pigment within a formulation, e.g. "Cadmium Red" for a color formulated with real, honest-to-goodness cadmium, and "Cadmium Red Hue" for color made with alternative pigments. In the case of cadmiums, cobalts, and other colors, the standard is a good thing. Artists should have some easy, accessible way of knowing when they're buying a substitute color, of different pigmentation than the original, and the "hue" nomenclature helps.

But here's where things get sticky. Under ASTM D-4302, manufacturers that use the new synthetic iron oxides would have to label their Burnt Sienna as "Burnt Sienna Hue," even though the synthetic color is highly comparable to the old, great pigments; more so, by some standards, than the real earths that are currently available. Manufacturers that choose to stick with ASTM D-4302, and not add another "hue" color to their ranges, will then stick with natural earths, of arguably lesser quality. Those that opt for the new synthetic earths, and that adhere to ASTM

Sometimes there's one way and one way only. While the production of pigments and colors has become quite sophisticated and technologically advanced, the only way to make the pigment used in the milling of Rose Madder Genuine is through a recipe first developed by colourman George Field in 1806. In addition to more technologically advanced processes, Winsor & Newton, in Wealdstone, England, is the only manufacturer to produce Rose Madder Genuine in accordance with the original process. Courtesy of Winsor & Newton.

D-4302, face the prospect of confusing their customers and hurting sales when they add a "hue" tag to their earth names, even though the new synthetic color will more closely match the older, original earth pigments.

What do you do? Some manufacturers are opting to, in good conscience, adhere to ASTM D-4302 wherever they can while avoiding name changes where an alteration in pigmentation results in little or no change in the traditional characteristics expected by artists.

• **How's our color bias?** Just about every color is biased in one direction or another. With reds, for example, a blue bias doesn't come because there's blue added to the pigment. It's simply a result of how light is reflected from the pigment toward the blue side of the spectrum. Quinacridones have a slight blue bias, and naphthols are biased toward the yellow. And you'll notice that many manufacturers are now producing phthalocyanine blue paints with a different bias, like red shade and green shade. There are lots of reasons for this, many of which will become clear in a later section. Right now, let's just say that it's critical to make certain that the color bias is true, and…

• **...Do we add to the balance of the spectrum?** At the risk of overworking an already tired analogy, pigments are chosen, in part, because of their ability to contribute to the balance of the "team." The ideal palette for the painter is one that allows an infinite array of mixing options all of the way around the spectrum. And the manufacturer offers those options by selecting pigments that "fit" into a balanced spectrum, with colors spaced evenly around the compass, and with a clean array of available bias being well represented.

• **Are we going to be stable and lightfast?** Today, the artist's palette is crowded with lightfast colors that weren't even a twinkle in a chemist's eye just a century ago. That said, there are still a few colors made that don't stand up to light and time as well as we'd like. In most cases, those colors are still produced because a suitable alternative hasn't emerged, or because artists continue to demand the

Even though it's made from a synthetic iron oxide, the rich tone and jewel-like translucency of the sample on the left is typical of the highest quality raw sienna. The natural earth raw sienna pigment on the right is denser, more opaque, and less like the original earth oxides that are becoming increasingly difficult to obtain.

color out of habit. Alizarin Crimson is an example; a color that rates as an ASTM "III" in lightfastness, it is still produced by a number of conscientious manufacturers, even though a more permanent alternative is now available. (More information on lightfast ratings and standards is coming up.) Permanent Alizarin Crimson has been available for a few years, and it's highly comparable in hue, chroma, bias, and transparency to the traditional color. And it's far more lightfast. Why is the traditional color still being made? Because artists demand it. Balancing the concerns with lightfastness with the demands (and habits) of the user is sometimes a challenge.

will pose the least degree of solubility or threat if inadvertently ingested by the artist.

(Note: I'm not one of those that advocates avoiding all products that raise any kind of health issues. If I were that over-cautious, I'd have to refuse to get in a car for the rest of my life. It is, however, wise to use all products with care. Cadmiums, because they can be absorbed much more readily through inhalation, should never be spray applied. And they should be handled with appropriate care, without pointing one's brushes in the mouth, or scrubbing your brushes while cleaning in the palm of the hand.)

• Do we match previous batches? Batches of pigment vary from one to another. The best manufacturers are using computers and colormetric measurement and all kinds of other technology to ensure that each batch of pigment that arrives meets specific standards that can be traced from batch to batch.

Once we've made the cut, we pigments head deep into the factory, where we meet our partners, linseed or safflower oil if we're going to be milled into oil color, acrylic polymer if we're bound to become acrylics, or gum arabic if we're headed for existence as watercolor.

These partners have been through a selection process just as rigorous as what we've just completed. The best linseed oil is naturally (rather than chemically) refined from the seeds of the flax plant, yielding an oil of pale color that will remain as stable as possible for years, decades, and gener-

• For the health of the user, are we as benign as possible? There's a complete chapter on health and safety ahead (Chapter 7), but for the time being, let's just say that, as we learn more about the potential health issues that accompany some products, reputable makers of color are choosing pigments that pose as few risks as possible. For example, cadmiums have come under the gun over the last decade or two. And with good reason. Cadmium can, if used carelessly, pose a health threat. But cadmium pigment can be produced in varying degrees of solubility. And the best manufacturers are making careful choices about which cadmium pigments to use, selecting those that

ations. The best acrylic polymer is selected from a wide range of options on the market, also being chosen for its clarity, its minimal shift in color upon drying, and its long-term stability. The best gum arabic is taken from a limited number of trees, in only certain areas upon the planet, that are proven to yield gum that, again, offers the greatest clarity and stability.

Monogamy is Better

Once we pigments make the cut, we get organized by "recipe" or formulation. Manufacturers arrive at their own unique formulations over the course of decades and, in the cases of firms like

The very best vehicles should remain stable for decades. Here is a collection of mediums and vehicles that dates back to the 1880s. Courtesy of Winsor & Newton.

Lefranc & Bourgeois (founded 1720) or Winsor & Newton (founded 1832), centuries. Because they include information, not only about ingredients, but about how those ingredients are milled, the formulations used by manufacturers are highly proprietary. Different formulations, even though they may include similar or the same ingredients, can yield products with very different working characteristics, stability, and potential for permanence.

There are lots of qualities that make a good formulation. And, in the case of choosing the right pigment for the color, it's almost always true that the use of a single pigment married to the vehicle is a much better choice than using multiple or mixed pigments. Monogamy is better for the color than polygamy. (Oh no! I've gone from a sports team metaphor to one about marriage!)

It's a fact: every time you mix colors upon your palette, you lose some of the brightness and bril-

liance of the original parent colors. The physical nature of mixing dictates that the pigments will, to some degree, cancel out some of the qualities of each other, and that green mixed from the parent blue and yellow will inevitably lose some degree of chroma or brightness. Depending upon the parent colors used, you can lose just a little chroma, or you can lose a lot. (More on that later.)

The same is true in the formulation of color and paint. A formulation with a single pigment means that you're starting with the brightest, truest character possible in that tube of color. Mixed pigment formulations are starting already from a slight disadvantage. Here's an example: a well-known manufacturer of acrylics produces a color called Alizarin Crimson Hue made from a pigment mix of quinacridone violet (which has a blue bias) and naphthol red (which has a yellow/orange bias). Now, at first, it makes a certain degree of sense that the two colors,

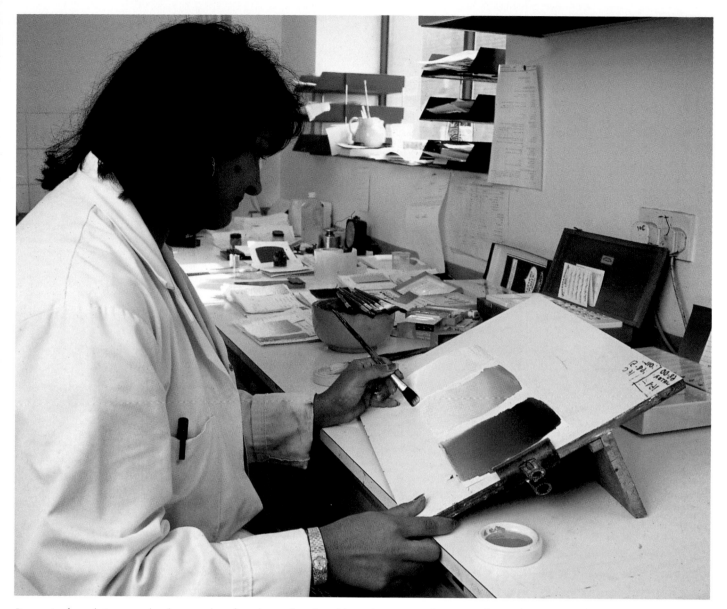

Pigments, formulations, and colors get their fair share of real-world test-drives as well as scientific analysis. Here, a lab worker is evaluating watercolor for a variety of working characteristics. Courtesy of Winsor & Newton.

when mixed, would yield a nice crimson with blue bias. But look at the bias of both parent pigments: blue and orange. What happens when you mix blue with orange? You get gray. And that is, in fact, what happens. The resulting crimson is flat, gray, and lifeless. Not at all like a true Alizarin Crimson, which has a rich, jewel-like glow, and that is formulated with a traditional pigment called 1, 2 dihydroxyanthraquinone lake (PR 83 is the Color Index Generic Name).

In this case, one reason for opting to formulate with mixed pigments is because true Alizarin Crimson doesn't offer a high degree of lightfastness. And the manufacturer has named the color a "hue," an indicator that it's not the real Alizarin deal. Nevertheless, this example serves to illustrate what

can happen when opting for mixed pigments in a formulation rather than using singles. Or a polygamous rather than a monogamous pigment and vehicle relationship.

Another manufacturer, rather than formulating a mixed "hue" substitute, has opted for investing the time and energy necessary to arrive at another solution. In addition to the traditional Alizarin Crimson (for those artists who just don't want a substitute and are willing to live with the lesser permanence), Winsor & Newton now offers Permanent Alizarin Crimson wherever possible within its ranges, a color that's similar in structure—and highly comparable in hue, chroma, and depth—to the original.

In some cases, pigments have to be mixed to achieve a given formulation; it's the only way to

The Alizarin Crimson Hue sample on the right is much duller and more gray than the genuine Alizarin Crimson on the left. The hue color is made from mixed pigments that have complementary color bias, producing a color that goes gray. The genuine color is made from a single pigment.

reach the color or hue that's evolved as the artist's ideal. But, wherever possible, single pigments make for a much superior spectrum. Single pigment colors are brighter and cleaner to begin with, and they make much brighter mixes. They broaden your creative options immeasurably.

How Much is Just Right?

Now that we've been matched to the proper formulation, we pigments are subject to another decision: how much.

There's a common misconception that more pigment in a tube of color is better. And that's true up to a point. But, just as too little pigment means no covering power, low tinting strength, and an increased potential for fading, too much pigment (and not enough vehicle) can mean compromised working characteristics and not enough vehicle to form a permanent, stable paint film.

Sadly, there are manufacturers that have played upon this concept that more pigment is better, even to an extreme, and have packed their tubes with so much pigment that the balance within the vehicle, and ultimately nothing less than the stability of the color, has been clearly compromised. This is color that has a much greater likelihood, at some point in the future, to crack and flake.

The very best color is formulated to achieve a fine balance between pigment and vehicle. That's true whether the pigment is being milled with oil, acrylic copolymer, or gum arabic for watercolors. And it's a balance that, while devilishly difficult to achieve, is fairly easy to understand. To understand how it's achieved, let's take a look at the ideal balance of pigment to oil.

Every pigment absorbs oil differently. Depending upon the shape of the pigment particle (small and smooth, or big and round, or big and jagged, and everything in between), oil must thoroughly fill or "wet" the pigment during milling. And the shape and size of the particle determines how much oil (and how much work or energy) is required to fully wet the pigment, bringing it into perfectly balanced suspension.

In well-milled color, every particle is perfectly suspended, fully surrounded by oil that, upon drying, forms a highly stable film. That's all there is to it.

Well, kind of. Things get complicated because every pigment is different. And sometimes pigment varies from batch to batch, so achieving the ideal suspension with each and every pigment requires extraordinary skill and experience.

Loosely paraphrasing a famous character in children's literature, it's fair to say that too much pigment, and there's not enough oil for a stable film. Too little, and the color lacks covering power and tinting strength. Just right, and you've got color with which it's an unadulterated joy to work.

Just as we've all been taught by Goldilocks, it's all in finding the right balance.

Okay, we're among the few and the chosen. We've been matched with our vehicle-partners. We've been formulated. Now, it's…

… Milling Time!

First we go into a big mixer. This isn't the actual milling; it's just a warm-up for the main event. Before going into the mill, we've got to be in some kind of

Formulations used by some manufacturers date back centuries. Here is a formulation book used in the 1880s by Winsor & Newton. Courtesy of Winsor & Newton.

Before being milled, pigment and vehicle are combined into a rough mixture. Courtesy of Winsor & Newton.

even blend, and a spin through the mixer does that.

Now into the mill. Fine color is made with a machine that's been used for centuries, a "triple-roll mill." These mills come in different sizes, depending upon how much color is being produced, and they look just like the name implies. There are three heavy rollers, across, betwixt, and between which the pigment and vehicle mixture passes. As the mixture goes between the rollers, the oil (if making oil color) or gum (if making watercolor) and pigment are "mashed" together, forcing vehicle into all of the little nooks and crannies that may exist upon the pigment particle. As milling progresses, and the pigment takes on more and more vehicle, it finally achieves the perfect dispersion and balance.

In the vast majority of cases, one trip through the mill isn't enough. To achieve complete dispersion, depending upon the mill, the vehicle, and the properties of the pigment, it can take as many as three, five, or even more passes.

The chemistry of acrylics doesn't require milling

upon a triple-roll mill. Different techniques, including good use of an industrial mixer, are employed for milling acrylic colors. But the principles and the goal are the same: to get the pigment into a balanced, stable suspension within the vehicle.

At the time of this writing, manufacturers are beginning to take advantage of new milling technologies and machines that are faster, that achieve better pigment-vehicle suspension, and that make an even better all-round product.

As an artist and user of the color, how do you tell if you're using well-milled paint? Much of it comes with experience. But even the novice can often tell by how the paint feels as it's brushed upon the surface. Is it smooth, with no excess vehicle? When you first squeeze oil color from the tube, do you get straight color, or do you get loose oil?

For a more experienced painter, the differences show up in other ways, as well. When you buy a tube of Cobalt Blue to replace the empty tube that you bought four months before, does it have the

An oil color is checked during a pass through the triple-roll mill. Courtesy of Winsor & Newton.

same body or viscosity as the first? Does the color mix consistently? As you use the color, are the true characteristics of the pigments apparent and usable?

It's often easier to see the results of poor, or inexperienced, milling. Poor milling of oil color shows up in tubes of paint that "settle," with gobs of oil rising to the top, and pigment falling to the bottom. Not only is it irritating to squeeze the tube and get nothing but oil, but it can indicate more serious problems, as well. Assuming that the formulation was correct

Here's another view of color (this time watercolor) being milled upon a triple-roll mill. Courtesy of Winsor & Newton.

Depending upon the characteristics of the pigment and the vehicle, different milling procedures are best suited to different colors. Here, watercolor is being milled upon a traditional cone mill. Courtesy of Winsor & Newton.

when the color was milled, the remaining mix (as the pigment has settled and the oil has separated) may not include enough oil to form a stable film upon drying.

Now that we've been milled—now that we've been embraced and enveloped by a layer of fine oil or gum or polymer—there's one more step before we go into tubes or pots or jars. On we go to...

... Quality Control

When color comes off the mill, it needs to be compared to previous batches. The fresh batch will be made to jump through hoops using a variety of gauges, tint cards, and measures. Each of these tests is designed to make certain that the current batch of color is comparable to previous batches in mass tone, undertone, chroma, viscosity, dispersion, and

all of the other variables that determine both the workability and the stability of the paint. Without this comparison control, there's virtually no way to make certain that the new color off the mill is going to be comparable (if not superior) to color that was purchased by the user six months, or six years, or even sixty years ago.

After taking this conceptual tour through the color mill, it should be clear that making paint is no simple task. Making the very best color comes with painstaking care and dedication, and only after years of experience. It's not coincidental that the best color makers on the planet have been making paint for decades and generations, if not centuries. It takes that long to get it right.

This isn't to say that it's a bad thing to experiment with making your own color (as I've seen countless

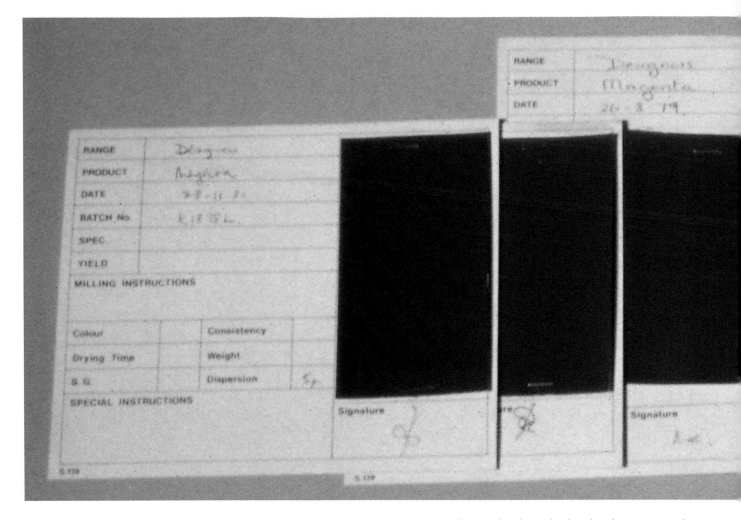

Makers of the finest color compare each batch to previous batches. Doing so ensures that each color embodies the characteristics that have been deemed most desirable by artists over the past decades or even centuries. Courtesy of Winsor & Newton.

people try). But do it not because you want better paint than you can get off the shelf or because you want color like the old masters (WWRD?), but because you want to better understand the constituents of your process. And always follow proper and rigorous safety precautions if you're doing anything with dry pigment.

As I said in Chapter 1, with the chemistry, the technology, and the pigments available today, the old masters would drool at the prospect of working with twenty-first century colors.

The Stable Film

The paint film is the Holy Grail of color. Upon drying on the painting surface, it's the film that ensures the stability of your expressive image. Without it, there's cracking, crumbling, and the inevitable disintegration of your hard work. In the previous section, we looked at how color is made in such a way to ensure that the paint can lead to a film that's as permanent as possible. But you're the one

who's using it. And if you want your image to last for a generation or two or ten, you've got to use it correctly. And you've got to understand how the film works.

The Oil Film

The chemical mechanism for the drying of linseed oil is astonishingly complex and still not fully understood. With that in mind, here's a simplified explanation of how your color goes from fluid paint to stable film:

Linseed oil doesn't dry through the evaporation of a solvent (as does acrylic polymer, or glue, or any of a number of other substances). It dries through a process called oxidation, in which, through exposure to the atmosphere, oxygen molecules come into contact with the paint and "link up" in a long-term marriage with individual oil molecules.

Here's where things get fun. Here's a simplified outline of what happens upon your painting surface: Each oxygen molecule doesn't marry itself to just one

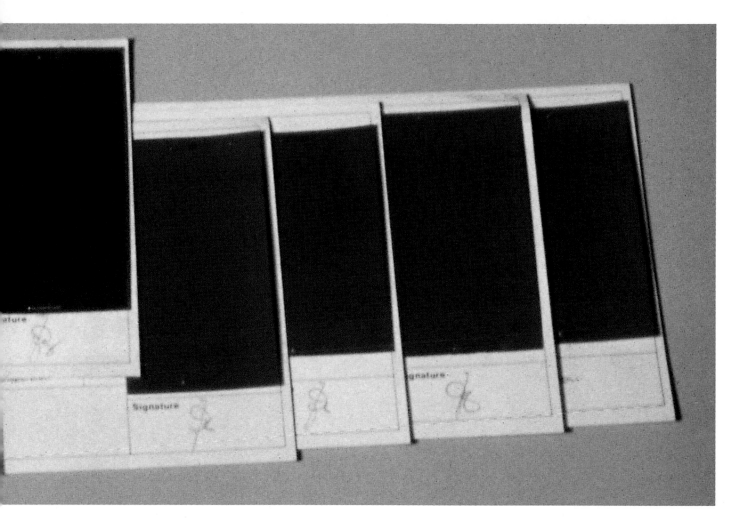

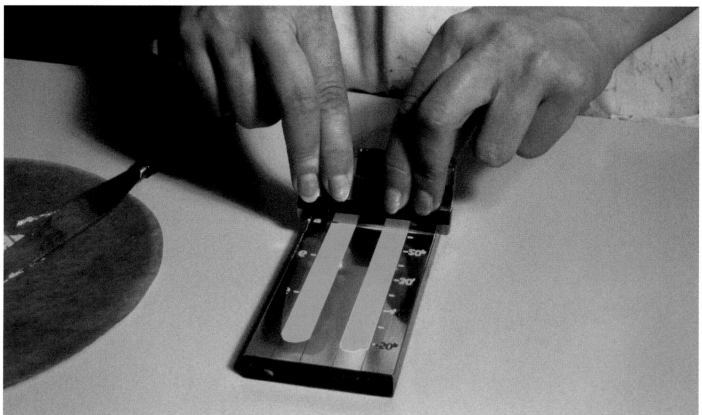

Once the batch of color has been milled, it needs to be tested for working characteristics and stability. Courtesy of Winsor & Newton.

The oil film, wet. While the illustrations above and on the opposite page are but rough approximations, they are accurate enough to provide a clear picture of what happens when oil color oxidizes and dries.

oil molecule; instead, the addition of oxygen at the ethylenic, or double bonds, on one molecule catalyzes a link with an adjacent oil molecule. In effect, the addition of oxygen launches the formation of an oil chain, creating a polymeric (a chemical term for a chain comprised of like or identical constituent molecules) lattice structure that effectively locks the pigment, and your creative expression, securely into place.

Anything that enhances (or at least doesn't hinder) the oxidation "marriage" makes for a stable film. Anything that gets in the way makes for a film that is progressively less secure. Here are some common mistakes that cause problems:

• **Overthinning.** Now that you can visualize the mechanism that turns fluid oil into that all-important film, you can visualize what happens when things interfere with that same process. The most common

The oil film, dry.

mistake made by painters is overthinning, or adding too much solvent, to the color. The mechanics of overthinning are simple. As you can see from the illustration on the next page, if you add too much solvent, spreading the oil molecules too far apart, they simply can't reach each other when it's time to oxidize, polymerize, and lock down the color.

Important Tip: If adding more than a splash of solvent to your color mix, it's wise to add painting medium, as well. Doing so will ensure that there's sufficient oil within the mix to form the stable film. In Chapter 5, we'll look more closely at the variety of mediums that can help you adjust the working characteristics of your color.

"Well, everybody else does it," is the most common response when presenting this to a group. And, yes, that's correct; the practice is widespread, to say the least. But, as my mom, your mom, and

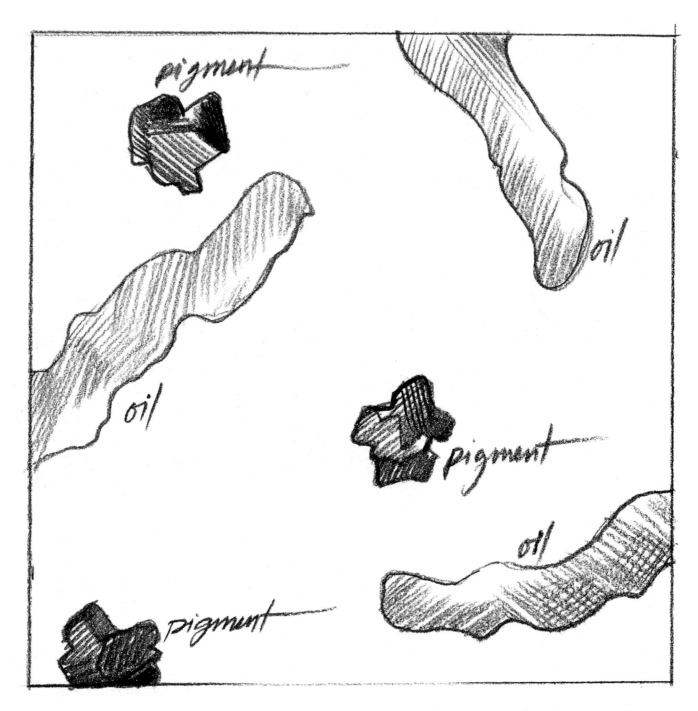

As you can see, overthinning simply spreads the linseed oil too far, preventing it from linking up to form the permanent film. Overthinning commonly results in color that is "underbound" and that never quite fully dries.

everybody else's mom has said, "Just because everybody else is doing it…"

The problem seems to come from two common misconceptions:

The first arises because underbound color often doesn't make itself known until somewhere down the road. So it's not uncommon for the painter to assume that, because you don't see any deleterious effects immediately, there won't be any later. Not so.

The second misconception seems to be that,

because you can get away with thinning color to a fairly fluid consistency when underpainting directly upon fresh, pristine gesso, you can do the same later in the painting. Again, not so. It only works when underpainting because of the absorbent nature of the gesso, which helps secure the color without the full benefit of the oil film. That absorbency isn't there to help later in the painting process, when the painter must depend upon the color forming stable layers all by itself, oil on top of oil.

• **Using poor-quality solvents.** I know how tempting it is to pick up that gallon of mineral spirits at your local hardware store. I know it costs only a few dollars, and that it's far less expensive than that artist-grade stuff at your favorite art materials store. One word: **Don't!** And there are some very simple reasons why.

The first is **purity of the solvent**. Hardware-grade solvents have been refined for use with house paints and colors that are formulated to last but a decade or two, at most. For painting houses, there's no real need to go to the expense required to remove every last bit of the extra flotsam and jetsam that can be floating around in the solution. But, if added to artists' colors, and, once the solvent has evaporated, all of that extra stuff is left behind and can get in the way of the formation of your paint film, leading to all kinds of problems later on. Artist-grade solvents have been purified to a high degree, ensuring that, upon evaporation, the solvent leaves nothing behind but oil and pigment.

This is a good time to say that, if you're using turpentine, make certain that it's fresh. Old, oxidized turpentine can leave a residue within the paint film and hinder the drying process. Turpentine should be stored in full bottles and in the dark.

The second reason is **your health**. Over the last few years, the wonders of modern chemistry have brought new, dramatically safer solvents to market. The days of exposure by oil painters to turpentine—which is, at best, unpleasant and, at worst, a real health hazard—are gone. "They (modern petroleum distilled solvents) have been getting better since they were first invented," observes Emma Pearce, Technical Services Manager for Winsor & Newton in Wealdstone, England, "and the good ones have been around for a long time. The aromatic content, which is the harmful part, keeps getting lower and lower."

Like the increase in the available choice of pigments, our community has seen direct benefit from developments in other industries. "Once again, nothing is made specifically for us," observes Robert Gamblin, of Gamblin Artists Colors. "We've chosen to use and package a specific solvent, that is actually quite expensive, because it's refined to such a degree that it's approved for running through food service equipment and for makeup formulations."

Two solvents that offer similar degrees of safety are Sansodor from Winsor & Newton and Gamsol from Gamblin Artists Colors. Both products have a threshold limit value (TLV) of 300 parts per million (ppm), a measurement of how much solvent is safe within your immediate environment. By contrast, the TLV for turpentine is 100ppm.

Citrus-based solvents have become steadily more popular within the art materials community over the course of the last decade. In the interest of safety and of stability, I strongly recommend against their use. First, many are not fully volatile and commonly contain products that remain behind, just waiting to sully your precious paint film. Second, even with the seemingly benign citrus odor, they are not without their own hazards and may well contain suspected toxins.

For oil painters who want to eliminate any and all exposure to aromatic solvents, water-mixable oil color has emerged as a real and viable alternative. While there are some trade-offs that come with the new chemistry, they are not as dramatic as you might imagine. And the elimination of solvent from the studio, while still being able to take advantage of the

The acrylic film, wet. Acrylic color dries as water leaves the mixture, allowing acrylic molecules to link up into a polymer chain, locking the pigment into place.

unique character of oil color, may well prove to be a real boon to students, colleges, and anyone wishing to work in a less noxious environment.

• Using inexpensive or household primers rather than real, honest-to-goodness artists' gesso. Even though you want a ground that offers some absorbency, too much can be almost as bad as too little. A ground that is too absorbent can, quite literally, suck the oil vehicle away from the pigment, a phenomenon known as "sinking." The moral of the story? Use good-quality gesso. How do you tell if your color has sunk? Within a matter of days, color that has sunk will appear flat and dull and will come free of the surface if the dull area is rubbed with a cloth that is lightly loaded with solvent.

How do you fix it? With a technique called "oiling out." In short, you want to replace the lost layer of oil. Use an appropriate vehicle (like Winsor & Newton Artists Painting Medium), rubbing it sparingly with a soft cloth into the sunken area of color.

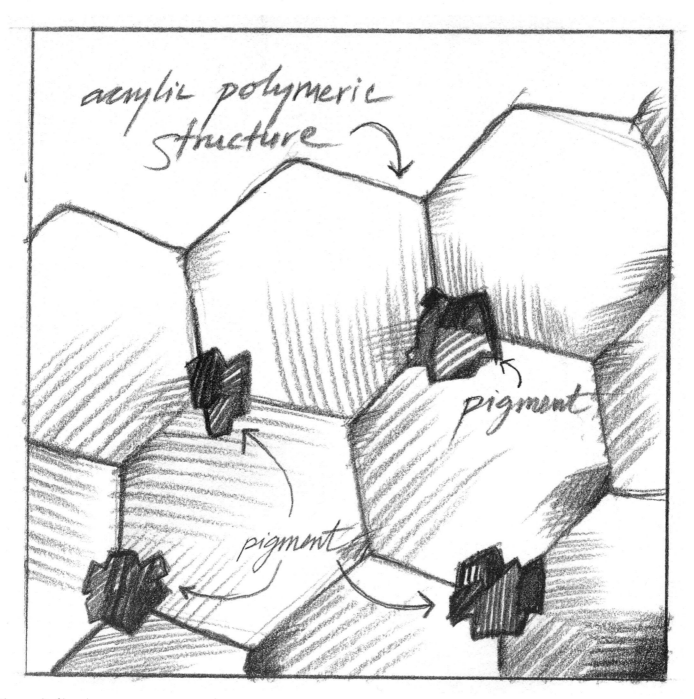

acrylic polymeric structure

pigment

pigment

The acrylic film, dry.

Wipe free any remaining vehicle and allow the painting to dry for a day or two. If any flat areas still remain, repeat the oiling out process until the surface regains a sheen that matches the "healthy" areas of color upon the painting.

• **Other mistakes that lead to the breakup of the oil oxidation marriage.** There are a few rules to remember about the application of oil color; things like "fat over lean," "thick over thin," "flexible over less flexible," and "slow drying over fast drying."

(We'll look at all of those in Chapter 5.)

The Acrylic Film

Some of the same principles—polymerization, purity of the partners—apply to the formation of a stable acrylic film "marriage." The primary difference between the formation of the acrylic film versus that of oil is that drying for acrylics is triggered by the evaporation of solvent from the mix. And, for acrylic colors, the solvent is water. And, just like with oil, if you understand how the film forms, you'll better understand how to use the color and keep it intact.

Right out of the tube or pot, your acrylic color includes these constituents: acrylic emulsion and pigment. (Remember what an emulsion is? It's a stable mixture achieved through chemical or mechanical means of substances that don't normally mix.) The emulsion is a mix of, among other things, acrylic polymer and water.

As water evaporates from the mix, the acrylic molecules come into contact, linking up to form a stable polymer chain and locking the pigment into place.

As with oil colors, the most common mistake made when painting in acrylics is overthinning. Makes sense, doesn't it? If the acrylic molecules are forced to share space with too much water, and are spread too far apart, they'll simply not be able to reach each other when the water evaporates and it's time to link up and form the film.

If all of this talk about how to take good care of your paint film isn't enough, just remember:

The Polymeric Limerick
There once was a painter named Rick
Who wanted his pigment to stick.
"Too much solvent!" he cried,
"My painting has died!
The film never locked down, polymeric!"

Watercolor
The gum arabic vehicle for watercolors serves a slightly different purpose than the vehicles for oils and acrylics. Rather than forming a self-contained structure to secure the pigment, the gum does three things:
• First, it coats and carries the color.
• Second, it brings working properties to the color.
• Third, it facilitates the stable adhesion of the color upon the surface.

The first two qualities can be said of oil and acrylic vehicles, as well. Regardless of your chosen medium, you want a vehicle in which the pigment is fully and evenly dispersed, and that carries it safely to your painting surface. You also want your vehicle to provide the proper working characteristics: stiff viscosity with smooth, buttery laydown for oils, and heavy or fluid body for acrylics. And, for watercolor, you want a vehicle that allows the color to go into immediate and consistent solution with water, that allows you to spread color freely, as well as to facilitate tight control, when desired. And it should do so with optical properties that might be described as richness, depth, and clarity.

The third quality is where things differ, for with watercolor, the paper surface becomes part of the structure that supports the color. And that's also, in part, why the quality of your paper is so critical. As the wash of color spreads across the surface of the paper, the solution of water, gum, and pigment settles into the topmost layer of the sheet. The absorbency of the paper is controlled by the added "sizing" within the sheet. Too little sizing, and the color is absorbed deeply into the body of the paper, and you lose the brilliance of your color. Too much sizing, and the color runs right off. Just right, and the paint is absorbed evenly into the topmost surface, giving you consistent control and maintaining the brilliance of the pigment. As water evaporates, your color is secured for the ages by the combined forces of the paper's surface structure as well as the adhesion of the remaining gum.

The best watercolor is milled with fine gum arabic mixed with a dollop of glycerin to serve as a humectant, keeping the color moist. As with oil color, watercolor that has been well milled will remain in suspension and won't settle within the tube. Poorly milled color, made from poor (or the wrong) ingredients can settle and sometimes harden within the tube. Fine color will remain soft and stable for years, sometimes even decades.

Some manufacturers use honey or other natural sugars as a humectant in watercolor. While there's a certain degree of romance that comes with milling honey with color, glycerine seems to be a more effective humectant, and honey has been shown to darken somewhat with age. Not to mention that honey may also attract unexpected guests.

Important Tip: If adding more than just a splash of water to acrylics, it's wise to add a splash of acrylic medium as well. Doing so will ensure that there's sufficient polymer within the mix to achieve that all-important stable film. In Chapter 5, we'll look more closely at the variety of mediums that can help you adjust the working character of your color.

Laurie Hines, an artist and friend, told me once of some surprising and unexpectedly colorful tenants when keeping a studio in the breathtaking, but bug-laden, environs of Hawaii. It seems that certain species of roaches were attracted to the leftover watercolor that lay waiting and delectable upon her palette at night. When morning came, and Laurie would chase the bugs back toward their hidey-holes, any that were unlucky enough to be overtaken and squashed would make a bright red (or blue or yellow or violet) splat upon the floor. I told Laurie that the strategic stomping and exudation of watercolor bugs was a painting process just waiting to be exploited.

Other Media

No matter what media you've chosen to work with and explore, the principles of the permanent film are the same as described on the previous pages. The color will hang around for the ages only if it's locked within a stable structural film (or in the case of waterborne media upon paper, within a combined structure of film and absorbent surface). This is true when working in pastel or in encaustic (melted wax) or egg tempera, or even in watercolor bugs (because of the ingested gum, there's good reason to expect that the color should be reasonably stable).

Now that you understand the essential principles behind a permanent paint film, you can tailor your working methods appropriately.

The Physics of Lightfast Color

As should now be obvious, permanence is much more than lightfast color. But the ability of a pigment to hold up under the violent assault of light energy is pretty important, too.

Light is energy. And light, even though it travels at an invariable speed (most of the time, at least, but that's a topic for another time and space), it does a number of different things as it dances and ricochets about.

Energy is made of little packets, or "quanta," of energy, which oscillate when moving around. When oscillating widely, they're called "infrared" energy. If the rate of oscillation tightens up a bit, they become red light. And if that red light happens to bounce into your eye, or my eye, or anybody's eye that happens to be sensitive to energy at that particular frequency, the "color cones" at the back of our eyeballs get stimulated, sending a specific signal up the optic nerve

to our brain. At that point, our brain says, "Hey! There's a red light!" or a Rome apple or marinara sauce or cadmium red on some painting.

Shorten up the oscillation even more, and it becomes visible as orange, then yellow, then green, then blue, then violet, and finally, ultraviolet. And our eyes are set up to be stimulated by all of those frequencies, recognizing color, until we get to the ultraviolet, which is where energy frequencies pass out of the visible spectrum and move on to x-rays and gamma rays and all kinds of cool, high-energy kinds of things.

If energy is bouncing into your eye, it's bouncing into other things too; most specifically, for the purposes of our discussion, a few select particles of pigment on the surface of a painting. Light from the sun is full of energy moving at all of the frequencies that make up the visible spectrum and more. (The same is true, in varying degree, of energy that comes from artificial light, like light bulbs.) When that energy smacks up against a particle of phthalocyanine pigment, for example, all of the energy except some at a very specific frequency is absorbed. The energy that isn't absorbed, and that bounces back out into the environment, may well find its way into your eye, stimulating your color cones, and making you say, "Hey! That's phthalo blue!"

To this point, our discussion on the topic of light and energy and pigment and eyes has been quite active, filled with words like "bouncing" and "smacking" and the like. That's on purpose, because the processes of light absorption and reflection and any subsequent stimulation are most active, indeed. So active and violent, in fact, that if a pigment particle lacks the required degree of structural integrity, it's likely to be blown to smithereens.

Take a look at the chemical diagram for phthalocyanine on the next page. It's a symmetrical, well-constructed piece of work. With all of those double bonds and rings reinforcing each other in a well-balanced structure, this is a pigment just made to withstand constant bombardment of energy. And as long as this molecular compound keeps the structure shown, it will continue to absorb and reflect energy in a way that characterizes phthalo blue. If this molecule is altered, or broken or blown apart, it will participate in the absorption and reflection of energy in a completely new way. It will no longer work like phthalocyanine blue. It will, in fact, fade.

And that's how pigment and color work. The

Christo & Jeanne-Claude, "Over the River, Project for the Arkansas River, State of Colorado," collage, 1999. 77.5 cm x 30.5 cm, and 77.5 cm x 66.7 cm, pencil, fabric, pastel, charcoal, crayon, and topographic map. © Christo, 1999. Photo by Wolfgang Volz.

pigments that have the requisite structural integrity to withstand the constant, brutal bombardment of light energy, like the phthalocyanines, and the umbers and cadmiums, are called "lightfast." Those that do not, like the one used to make genuine alizarin crimson, crack and fall to bits under the assault. They fade away and are called "fugitive."

(In the next chapter, we'll talk about how different pigments and paints are rated for permanence. We'll also look at how the artist can make the best use of specific pigments and their individual qualities, along with the working differences between paints called "artists' quality" and those produced for students.)

Should every image or every painting be produced with the express intent that it lasts for centuries? That's not for me to answer. Certainly, there's been lots of artwork—in particular over the last twenty-five years—that has been produced with the understanding that it will be transitory. The remarkable installations of Christo and Jeanne-Claude are an example of long years and astonishing energy invested into ephemeral projects, each one created with the understanding that the finished installation will be in place for but short period of time. When asked why the works remain for only a few days, Jeanne-Claude says, "It's much like with childhood. Because you know it will not last, it is all the more precious. We want to endow our work with that quality of love and tenderness for what we know will not be here tomorrow."

But even Christo and Jeanne-Claude can't avoid the permanence issue. The chief strategy for funding their installations is in the production of working drawings and collages, works that serve to help in the conceptualization, design, and engineering process, but that also are sold to museums and collectors. "But they (the drawings and collages) are not the project," says Jeanne-Claude. "They are about the project. Just like the photographs of the completed work are not the work, they are about the work."

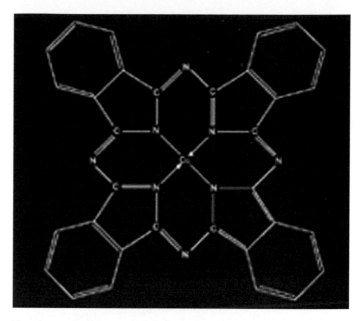

The chemical structure of phthalocyanine pigment. Courtesy of Winsor & Newton.

The decision about intended permanence rightly rests with the artist. But there has also been a huge volume of work that has proven to be highly transient, and quite unintentionally. And that doesn't include the countless paintings, handprints, and color cut-outs made by children that are fading into oblivion upon the walls of parents and grandparents the world over. Childhood, like the work of Christo and Jeanne-Claude, may be precious and fleeting. But there's every reason to expect the relics that follow in their wake to be of value and to be long lasting.

Whether your concern with paints and colors comes exclusively out of your interests as an artist or teacher, or if there's parental sentiment, as well, then there's no substitute for understanding what makes permanent color. When your intent is to produce work that will last past your, or your children's, lifetime, then a clear understanding of the paint film, how it forms, and how pigment remains intact under the daily assault from light will help you do exactly that.

Chapter 4

Making the Grade: The Standards for Artists' and Student Colors

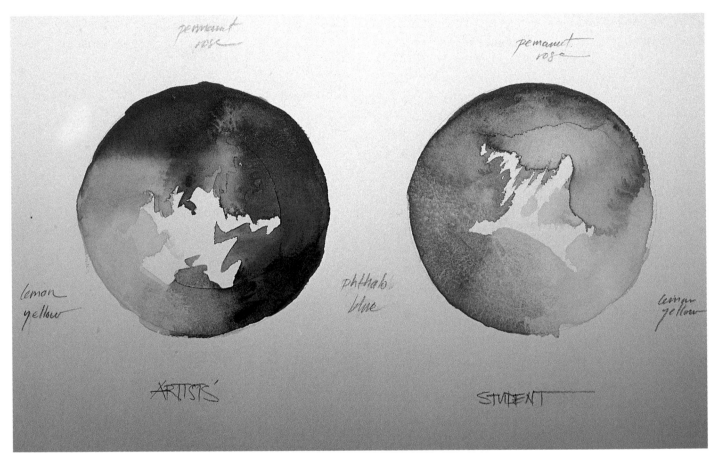

The color wheel on the left was made with the highest quality, artist-grade colors. The one on the right was made with quite reputable student-grade paints. The differences in color strength, brilliance, mixing, and pigment characteristics can be dramatic.

Some years ago, while I was working in an art materials store, a tall gentleman approached me. The brim of his wide cowboy hat was pulled low over his eyes. He wore a cream-colored down vest and a plaid flannel shirt stretched across his ample girth. Before he said a word, I was certain that whatever passed his lips would come out with a drawl. Sure enough, he stopped before me, opened his mouth and proceeded to transform each vowel he spoke into two or three.

I listened for a moment, and then shook my head. After answering questions from thousands of artist-customers over the previous years, I knew that there was always some new query waiting to take even the most experienced salesperson by surprise. But this one got me.

"I'm sorry," I said. "You want to do what?"

"I need somethin' so's I can make me a mold of a fish head."

My first impulse was to say "Well let's just head back to the fish-head-molding department," but I didn't.

"Please forgive me," I replied, hoping that he wasn't carrying a dead trout in his pocket. "This isn't a request that we get every day. Let's think for just a minute, and I'm sure we can come up with something."

"And then I need somethin' to paint it with."

I peered at him. "The real head or the molded one?"

There are lots of pleasures that come with working in the art materials community. The industry operates within a unique intersection, constantly looking for ways to integrate the methods of science with the processes of art and aesthetics. There is a steady tide of unique challenges and, on occasion, exhilarating solutions. And there is always something new to learn; it's a community full of interesting problems and unexpected opportunities.

There are always great questions from the people using the products, questions that often betray the unique, inventive uses to which the products are put and that offer the very real opportunity to learn something fun in the process of digging for an answer. "I'd like to grind my own watercolors. Is there something I can add to the mix that will be a good preservative?" (From one very dedicated and conscientious painter.) "Which watercolor paper has the most even surface sizing, and which will take the most scrubbing or abuse?" (From two architecture students who proceeded to buy and then rigorously test ten or fifteen different watercolor sheets.)

There are also the questions that come up over and over again: "Can you paint oils over acrylics?" (or vice versa?) "What's it mean when it says 'hue' on the tube?" "How long do oil paintings have to dry?" "How soon can I varnish my oil painting?" All of these (and more) are questions that, if I do my job, will be answered during the course of this book. But what's the most oft-asked question? Clearly in the top three, and maybe the all-time winner on the hit-parade of paint and color queries is this: "How come one tube costs $4 and another one costs $24?"

The Cost of Color

Manufacturers of artists' quality colors categorize the pigments used in groups, or "series," and price them accordingly, with "series one" being the least expensive, going up to "series five" or "six." After reading this far into the book, the reason for this strategy should be reasonably clear. Some pigments are more costly than others to acquire, while others require more involved milling procedures, and each

of those conditions obviously adds to the cost of production.

It's worth saying here that when comparing prices within a single range of artists-grade colors, any discrepancy in cost does not imply that one color is better than another. Even though one color may cost four or five times as much as another, both have been milled to the same standards and levels of dispersion. It's just that it costs more to get some pigments to those standards. And there are certainly cases when the less expensive color can be the very best color choice for a given application. Whenever possible, choose your colors based upon your need for the qualities of opacity, color bias, tinting strength, and granulation rather than cost.

There is another element that comes into play when evaluating the cost of color. Up to now, we've been discussing the standards that are used to mill color of the very highest quality. There are colors produced, however, to different standards, that result in lower cost. And, while lower cost colors can be perfectly workable in some circumstances, you should understand how they differ in performance and quality when compared to artists' quality ranges.

What's New With Hue? Comparing Artists' and Student Colors

By now it should be clear that making the finest quality color is an expensive proposition—and that expense is often a deterrent to students or hobbyists. So, manufacturers are constantly faced with the challenge of how to produce colors that will fit within tighter budgets while not sacrificing the working characteristics too severely. It's not easy.

Because the most critical ingredient in the color, the pigment, is also the most expensive, any adjustment in pigment load or milling is the most feasible way to adjust the cost. It's also the quickest way to compromise the working qualities. So a student-grade color, if it's to have reasonable working properties, can't be too low in pigment content.

To achieve a reasonable balance between price and working integrity, the best manufacturers select pigments for student colors that are low in cost and that can be milled quickly into a stable dispersion. These are typically pigments like the sienna and umber earths (both natural and synthetic), and synthetic organics, like phthalocyanine, quinacridone, and arylamide. These are low enough in cost that sufficient pigment can be included in the formulation to make color with reasonable working character and moderate price. Colors made with genuine cadmium and cobalt are often not included, because of their much higher cost. Student-grade colors are typically offered at a single price, rather than in the multiple series typical of artists' colors.

"Hue" colors are usually offered in student ranges as replacements for the genuine cadmiums and cobalts. What's the difference? A hue color has been formulated (often with mixed instead of single pigments) to offer chroma, value, and hue that approximates the genuine color. Because, however, the alternative color is made with pigments (almost always a synthetic organic) that differ in color bias and relative opacity from the genuine color, they mix quite differently than the original. Here's a bottom line on hue colors: they're not bad; just different. In some instances, the hue may even be a better choice than the original. Naphthol, perylene, and pyrrole are pigments commonly used in making cadmium red hue, and, when well-milled, each makes a bril-

liant red of superb clarity. Just understand that, when used as a "hue" color, they approximate a more costly pigment while offering their own mixing and working characteristics.

For the experienced—yet budget-minded— connoisseur of color, there are often superior (and not much more costly) choices to "hue" colors that can sometimes be found in a single pigment artists' range, for example, Pyrrole Red and Napthol Red, both of which are magnificent single pigment colors. And both of which, because of the relative pigment cost, are not much more expensive than many "cadmium red hues" upon the market, "hues" that don't approach the brilliance, clarity, and chroma of the single pigment Pyrrole and Naphthol colors. There are also fine oranges, yellows, and blues available in single pigment colors, which cost much less than cadmiums and cobalts, but not much more than "hue" alternatives in student ranges.

The bottom line? Know your pigments and read the labels for the pigments used in formulation.

Cadmium: An Endangered Species?

Until the early portion of the twentieth century, the finest red available was Vermilion. It offered great brilliance, warmth, and clarity, and it had been used by the Chinese, the Egyptians, and all of the great Renaissance guys; in short, by any artistic-type who was anybody. But Vermilion, being a form of mercuric sulfide (HgS), is a big-time health hazard. And it is, quite justifiably, no longer being produced. Luckily for your palette and mine, about the time Vermilion was being phased out, cadmiums had found their place in the artistic cosmos, offering an alternative of great brilliance, clarity, and opacity.

Now, at the beginning of the twenty-first century, with a variety of heavy metals being scrutinized as potential hazards, will the same thing happen to cadmium? It's impossible to say, but there's no question that worldwide use of cadmium is in decline. And the art materials industry takes advantage of pigments that are produced for much more extensive application in other markets. Cadmium, being used primarily in the plastics industry, is no exception. At the time of this writing, within university and college studios across North America, there is increasing scrutiny being brought to bear upon the use of cadmiums. Will they be regulated out of production? Or will the market simply move to other alternatives? Who knows?

There is some health concern associated with cadmiums, although there is also no end of debate about how much. Cadmiums have been shown to pose some risks if dissolved and absorbed into the system. In an effort to minimize risk and to make colors that pose as little threat as possible, reputable makers of artists' colors make use of cadmium pigments that have been proven to be of very low solubility.

Even so, it's wise to use cadmium colors with care and caution. Don't point your brushes in your mouth. Don't clean your brushes by mashing them into the palm of your hand with soap. Don't paint with your fingers. And, in particular, avoid any kind of spray application with cadmiums.

So, what comes next? There's been an explosion in the number of available red pigments during the last few decades. Will one of those prove to be a viable alternative to cadmiums, just like cadmium was to Vermilion? To date, there is no other pigment that matches cadmium in hue, opacity, and mixing characteristics (although the organic pyrroles and some of the naphthols come closest). I remain hopeful that, as pigment chemistry continues to evolve, there will be a viable alternative that emerges.

Cadmium Red

Cadmium Red Hue

Cadmium Yellow

Cadmium Yellow Hue

On this and the following two pages, an example of genuine Cadmium and Cobalt artists' colors is on the left, while their "hue" counterparts in a student range are on the right. Notice the difference in opacity. The student colors are made from pigment that approximates the hue of the original color at lower cost. While they mix and perform quite differently—and even though the naming convention can be confusing—the "hue" counterparts are not necessarily poor colors; they're just different.

Cobalt Blue

Cobalt Blue Hue

Mixture made from Cobalt Blue and Cadmium Yellow

On the left, the green mixed from genuine Cobalt Blue and genuine Cadmium Yellow is a dark, opaque, somewhat gray mixture. The green mixed from the student-grade, "hue" counterparts is brighter and transparent. Why? Because the "hue" colors are milled from synthetic organic colors that, by virtue of their physical nature, are brighter, more transparent, and make brighter mixes. Depending upon their intended use, there are occasions when either mixture might well be the best choice.

Mixture made from Cobalt Blue Hue and Cadmium Yellow Hue

	Artists' Colors	Students' Colors
Pigment load	Formulated with as much pigment as is necessary (usually regardless of cost) to achieve the ideal mixing and working properties.	Formulated with sufficient pigment to offer dependable, if not ideal, working properties.
Milling	Milled to achieve thorough and complete dispersion of pigment within the vehicle, regardless of resources required.	Milled quickly (where possible), using pigments requiring minimal resources, to offer dependable stability and working properties.
Price	Priced in series, according to pigment. Quality of color more important than cost.	Often priced at a single level; sometimes with a second series for genuine cadmiums and cobalts.
True pigment character	Formulated to offer ideal qualities of opacity/transparency, color bias, and tinting strength for every color in the range.	Formulated to offer dependable qualities of opacity/transparency, color bias, and tinting strength for a more limited range. "Hue" colors usually offered as alternatives to genuine cadmiums or cobalts.
Fillers or extenders	Minimal use of additives and only for the purpose of improving viscosity and working properties. Extenders used only to bring down excessive tinting strength of colors like those made from phthalocyanine.	Fillers or extenders used only when necessary to moderate price. Because lower cost pigments are used, good quality student colors require a minimum of fillers. Watch out for colors that are priced "too good to be true." They generally are. There are colors on the market that, in the interest of selling at the lowest price possible, have been formulated with far too much extender, compromising the stability, permanence, and working character of the color.
Permanence	Formulated to offer the best possible lightfastness (depending upon color) and stability of film.	Permanence of many student colors, when used appropriately, is often quite good. Many of the pigments used in formulation, even though of lower cost, offer superior lightfastness. Again, watch out for colors that are priced "too good to be true."
Spectrum	Broad and complete spectrum of colors, sometimes in excess of a hundred within a given range. The ideal spectrum is well balanced and allows the artist an almost infinite array of mixing options.	Good student ranges offer a balanced, while more limited, spectrum.

The table on the opposite page outlines the fundamental differences between color made to be the very best and those that are made to fit within the confines of the student budget.

There are a number of student ranges of color on the market that offer dependable performance and that represent a workable entré to the pleasures of painting. There's no substitute, however, for true artists' quality colors, where superior tinting strength, pigment characteristics, and working properties can make a profound difference in the success and the pleasures that are found in painting. And that's true whether you're an experienced pro or a raw beginner.

More on Permanence: ASTM and Manufacturer Ratings

After reading the previous chapter, you should have developed a clear understanding of what makes the most stable, permanent color. But how do you translate that information into choosing colors off the shelf?

The American Society for Testing and Materials (ASTM) has established standards for lightfastness of artists' colors. The ASTM subcommittee on Artists' Paints and Related Materials is comprised of some remarkably bright and dedicated men and women, many of whom have devoted their lives to the development and production of the finest, most permanent products for artists that money can buy. The committee is made of manufacturers, chemists, artists, and educators.

Here, in short, is a description of the ASTM standard on lightfastness: colors are tested by reducing, or tinting, to a level of 40 percent reflectance by the addition of titanium. "Reflectance" means the amount of light reflected from the color swatch. Watercolors aren't tested with added titanium, because the white of the paper surface is used for its reflective quality.

Once the color has been tinted, it's subjected to a variety of tests, both in direct sun as well as in a machine called a xenon-arc fadeometer, in which the samples are subjected to light in a manner that simulates exposure over years and decades and even centuries. Depending upon how the color fares during testing, the ASTM standard is applied, rating the color for fastness to light.

The colors are rated on a scale of I to V (depending upon the medium), with I being the highest lightfastness available. Ratings of both I and II are consid-

ered permanent for artists' use, while III and above are considered fugitive, in degrees ranging from moderate to color-that-disappears-before-your-very-eyes.

Color made from pigments that qualify for either an ASTM I or II rating, when applied with appropriate methods and exhibited under normal interior lighting, can be expected to remain intact and fade-free for generations—centuries, even, if well taken care of.

In the case of colors milled from mixed pigments, the overall ASTM rating is applied based upon the rating for the least lightfast pigment in the mixture. For example, if a color is milled using an earth color

How Much Is Enough?

There is truly an astonishing amount of technical information available about painting and painting materials. And this book is intended, in its own modest way, to provide a basic, but secure, foundation for readers interested in how to use their materials in the most productive and safest ways possible. For any and all that may be interested in more detailed information, there are a number of superb resources that offer a wealth of technical data about pigments and the other constituent parts of color. The Painter's Handbook, by Mark Gottsegen (Watson Guptill, NY, 1993.) is an excellent source (and, at the time of this writing, Mr. Gottsegen is the chairman of the ASTM subcommittee on Artists' Paints and Related Materials). Another dependable text is the old standby The Artist's Handbook, by Ralph Mayer (Viking, New York, revised edition, 1991). In the UK a fine resource is Artists' Materials: Which, Why and How, by Emma Pearce (A&C Black, London, 1992).

A small, but invaluable book (and one that I carry in my briefcase all of the time, because you never know when someone may ask you for the Latin name of the Larch tree used in the production of Venice Turpentine [Larix decidua]) is Painting Materials, by Rutherford J. Gettens and George L. Stout (Dover Publications, New York, first published by D. Van Nostrand, 1942).

To learn more about the standards used in reference to artists' materials, contact ASTM at: American Society for Testing and Materials, 100 Barr Harbor Drive, West Conshohocken, PA 19428-2959 (or more information can be found at www.astm.org).

of lightfastness I in combination with a modern organic pigment of lightfastness II, the finished color in the tube would be labeled with lightfastness II.

As you know very well by now, permanence is more than just being lightfast. So, the very best color manufacturers provide information about the permanence of the whole mixture—vehicle stability as well as the lightfastness of the pigment—and how the entire mixture is expected to withstand the passing rigors of time. On the tube or color chart, look for a rating for overall permanence. Manufacturers use a variety of codes, from a series of stars (****), to letters, but they identify their colors in general, as meeting some standard for permanence. The best manufacturers provide information about how their colors meet ASTM standards, as well as their own.

Later in this chapter, under the heading Reading the Labels and Literature, we'll detail how to interpret the information provided by reputable manufacturers.

Testing Your Own Color

You don't have to take my word for it. Testing your own colors for lightfastness and stability is a worthy exercise. Here are some tests you can try:

Testing for Lightfastness

On a canvas board (for oils or acrylics) or strip of watercolor paper (for watercolors or gouache), lay down swatches of colors you use regularly. Apply the swatches in a vertical row, and try to apply the color with a thicker film (mass tone, about which we'll discuss more later) on the top portion of the stroke, pulled down to a thin, more transparent film below (undertone). The reason for trying to get two distinctly different thicknesses of film is because some colors are considered permanent in a thick film and less so in a tint, or thin film. Be sure to label the colors by name.

Now, cut a strip of thick paper or board longer than the total length of all of your swatches. The paper or board needs to be heavy enough to prevent light from passing through. Tape the strip over one half, or one side, of the length of the swatches, and place the board in a window that gets plenty of sun. Then let it sit. And sit. And sit some more, over the course of weeks and months.

Periodically (every few weeks), take the board from the window and lift the strip to compare the side that's been covered to the side that's been exposed to sun. You'll see that colors which rate an

It's easy to test your own colors for lightfastness. While this home-made procedure won't give you quite the accuracy or control of a standardized procedure, it will give you some clear indications about the colors you use regularly.

This kit made by Golden Artist Colors gives specific instructions for lightfast testing.

ASTM I or II will have changed little or not at all. And, if you're using colors that are prone to fading, you'll see the difference. If you're using fluorescent colors, or liquid dyes like those made by Luma or Dr. Martin's, you'll notice fading in a matter of days.

For a more formal test, Golden Artist Colors produces a lightfast test kit that includes more specific instructions and control swatches.

Film Testing

My friend Laurie Hines is an education advisor for Winsor & Newton. One day, while teaching a workshop on colors to a group of college students, she mentioned having recently been to a museum in Southern California and how she couldn't help but notice that paintings done by a group of artists from a single geographic area (I won't say where) were in bad shape. The paintings were a few centuries old, and the surfaces had myriad cracks and had "eggshelled" badly. Strolling to a nearby room, she noticed paintings by a group of Dutch painters from the same time period as in the previous room. The Dutch paintings were smooth, stable, and had minimal cracking. "Those old Dutch guys knew how to paint!" she exclaimed.

I happened to be in Laurie's audience that day, and, after the program, we decided upon (with apologies to a well-known sports drink pitchman) a rallying cry for painters: "Be Like Van Eyck!" She's right. Those guys really knew how to put on the color.

So, if you're painting in oils (we'll address the same for acrylics later), and you *want* your color surface to crack, eggshell, ripple, or to never fully dry, what should you do? For fun and some valuable edification, here are some sample tests that will help you better understand the limits of your colors:

• Apply a thick film of color and allow it to set until tacky. Then, mix color to apply as a second layer, only load the color with solvent. And I mean really load it up. Apply the second layer of color and allow to dry. There are a number of things that will happen with this film, some of which you'll notice fairly soon: the top layer won't bond securely to the layer below, and the film will seem to take forever to completely dry. In fact, it probably won't. And when it gets as close to dry as it can get, it will be much more brittle than the thicker layer below, leading to cracking a few years, or weeks, ahead.

What have you done with this exercise? You've violated at least two critical rules for painting: fat over lean (the rule for applying more oil-rich layers over less oily layers), and you've underbound the color by adding too much solvent. You've also put a thin, quick-drying layer over a thicker, slow-drying layer.

This film of color has been overthinned and underbound. With this close-up, you can see that the color is loosely spread and will be prone, over time, to disintegration.

• For this next example, you have to be patient; like on the scale of months or a year-or-two patient. Apply a thick layer of a safflower oil-based white, like Zinc White, onto canvas. (Check the tube to determine the vehicle. Reputable manufacturers will tell you if you're using a white that's been milled with linseed or safflower oil.) Allow to dry until tacky. And be patient; safflower oil colors dry more slowly than those milled with linseed oil. After the layer of white has become firm, apply a second layer of color. For the second layer, choose a color like Raw Umber or Prussian Blue, both of which are fast-drying. Over time, you'll see that the top layer is less stable and will become highly prone to cracking.

So, what's happened here? We've broken another rule, this time the one about how fast-drying colors shouldn't be applied over slow-drying colors. For most painters and most techniques, with today's technology and better quality colors, this rule hardly ever crops up. Except in extreme cases. And we've just created an extreme case.

Safflower oil and poppy oil are called semi-drying oils. Why? Because they dry very slowly. Why is safflower oil used in milling white oil color? Because it's lighter in color and less prone to yellowing than linseed oil, and that's obviously pretty important with white pigment. And when white is mixed with other colors, the effects of the slower drying safflower oil are mitigated. But, when a safflower oil white by itself is used extensively in underpainting, bad things can happen, like cracking of subsequent layers, especially when laying a fast-drying color on top.

• For the next exercise, mix stand oil with your color. Not a little; a lot. Really a lot. Then apply the paint. Again, be patient; stand oil slows drying, so it will take a while to see the results, but during the course

A paint film that has wrinkled upon drying. Adding more medium or drying oil than is necessary can cause the paint film to expand and contract in less than uniform ways.

of oxidation, you'll see that the film begins to change and shift. In fact, it will go wrinkly.

The moral of this exercise story? Feel free to use mediums to adjust the working properties of your color, but use only as much as you need and then no more. Stand oil is a wonderful medium; it improves the flow of the color, levels out after brushing, and is superb for glazing and for creating fine detail. But

Another fun fact: *The physical properties and the chemistry of the pigment can affect the drying speed of the paint film. Some colors dry faster than others. Raw Umber, for example, contains manganese as a tag-along element, and manganese acts as a catalyst for oxidation, speeding the drying. So, by applying a fast-drying color over the slow-drying white, we've set up a situation for paint-film failure.*

Yet another fun fact: *When oils dry, they undergo a variety of dimensional changes. They swell, they contract. And, as mentioned earlier, they get fat and put on weight as oxygen is incorporated into the molecular lattice structure. Alun Foster, Chief Chemist for Winsor & Newton in Wealdstone, England, says "Semi-drying oils, such as safflower and poppy oil, undergo greater dimensional changes than linseed oil. While a safflower oil-based white is perfectly appropriate for use in normal applications and mixing, it is not suitable for extensive use in underpainting. The movement of the film can lead to cracking in the layers applied above."*

Be like van Eyck! The proper application of finely milled oil color can leave a paint film that holds up for centuries. (Detail of "The Arnolfini Wedding," by Jan van Eyck (c. 1390-1441), 1434, oil (with some tempera) on panel. National Gallery, London. Courtesy of Erich Lessing/Art Resource, NY.

adding too much means that you've created a mixture that's out of "balance." The stand oil and the linseed oil dry differently enough, and the differences in dimensional shifting will become clearly apparent in the surface of the film.

The point to these exercises, obviously, is to help you understand the implications of poor technique. You'll remember better what to do right if you've done it wrong and understand the reasons. You'll be like van Eyck.

For painters in acrylic colors, the effects of technique aren't always quite so serious. Now that we've gotten through the first fifty years with acrylics, and manufacturers are learning how to make better and better color with polymer emulsions, acrylics are proving to be more forgiving than oil colors. The real faux-pas when painting with acrylics is in overthinning. If you like, try the first exercise outlined on page 73, with a water-laden film of color applied over a thick, straight-out-of-the tube layer of paint. You'll find that the second layer dries unevenly and is

easily scraped free. Not a good scenario for a painting that aspires to longevity.

Reading the Color

There are specific qualities that determine how the color works. Although we've already talked about many of them, it doesn't hurt to outline them in some detail. Here are some illustrated characteristics you should remember when choosing your colors and building your palette:

Mass Tone and Undertone

These are terms that describe the appearance of the color, depending upon application. Mass tone is how the color appears in a thick layer. It's in this thick layer that the pure color is at its most dense and opaque. The undertone describes how the color appears in a thin layer. This is where some of the more subtle, but critical, characteristics of the color become visible. The relative transparency, or opacity, shows up clearly in the undertone, as does the color bias (see also page 77), as well as its tendency toward granulation (see also page 80). Often a color will appear dense and dark in its mass tone, but reveal itself to be bright and high chroma in its undertone.

Mass tone　　　　**Mass tone**

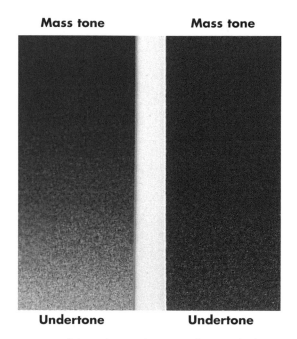

Undertone　　　　**Undertone**

The mass tone of the color can be seen when applied in a thick layer. The undertone is the color in a thin film. On the left is Winsor Red Deep, a color from the Winsor & Newton Artists' Oil Colour range and milled from a perylene red pigment. On the right is Genuine Cadmium Red Deep. Notice how the colors differ from each other in both mass tone and undertone.

Cadmium Red Light, a yellow shade red

Pyrrole Red, an unbiased red

Permanent Rose, a blue shade red

Mass tones of Cadmium Red Light (upper left), Pyrrole Red (upper right), and Permanent Rose (lower).

Color Bias

Pigments and colors can be shaded toward different parts of the spectrum, and this shading—or bias—can produce effects both subtle and dramatic. For example, Cadmium Red Light is shaded toward the warm, or yellow; Permanent Rose is shaded toward the cool, or blue; and a Pyrrole Red may close to a true, unbiased red. (See the illustration on the opposite page.)

Often, it's in the undertone of the color that the bias becomes most clearly apparent. (See the illustration below.)

As shown in the illustrations on the following pages, the bias of the color is not only apparent within individual colors, but it can have a profound effect upon mixing.

Transparency and Opacity

There's a common misconception that colors are made more or less transparent by virtue of how much pigment is in the mix. As should be abundantly clear by now, with expertly milled artists' quality color, transparency, or opacity, is a result of the physical properties of the pigment, not the pigment load. Some pigments, when viewed through a microscope, appear dense and opaque. And those qualities show up in the color. So, when the paint is well-milled, it takes on the opaque nature of the pigment. Other pigments, such as the phthalocyanines and the synthetic iron oxides mentioned before, when viewed through a microscope, appear to have the translucent quality of stained glass. And that characteristic shows up in the color, as well.

This property is true of good color even in mediums that are commonly considered to be more transparent, such as watercolor or alkyd oil color. While these mediums both tend toward transparency to a greater degree than oils or acrylics, they both include colors that exhibit more opacity than others.

The quality of pigment transparency or opacity affects more than the optical character of the individual color. Transparent colors mix much differently than do opaque (see the cadmium/cobalt mixing samples on pages 68 and 69). Below are color comparisons that illustrate a few of the fundamental differences between opaque and transparent.

Granulating Colors

Because of how the pigment spreads and swims during painting, this quality applies to watercolor

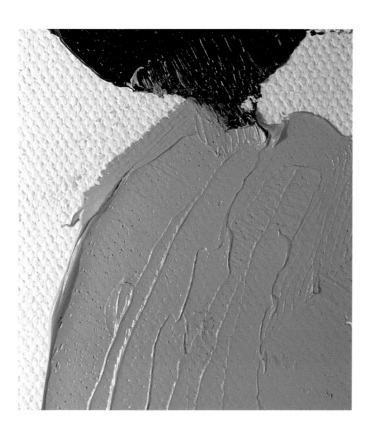

Phthalo green blue shade (left) and Phthalo green yellow shade (right). The bias of a color (how it's shaded toward another color in the spectrum) is often more apparent in the undertone, or in a tint with white. These two phthalo greens don't appear much different in their mass tone, but tinted with twenty parts white to one part color, it becomes apparent how very different they are.

Orange mixed from a cool red and a cool yellow.

The brightest mixes are going to come from colors that have a color bias that do not cancel each other out (such as the mixed pigment Alizarin Crimson hue shown on page 44). Mixing a warm red with a cool yellow produces a grayer mix, while the above mixture of Permanent Rose and Transparent Yellow (Azo)—both of which are on the cool side of the spectrum—creates a bright, vibrant secondary.

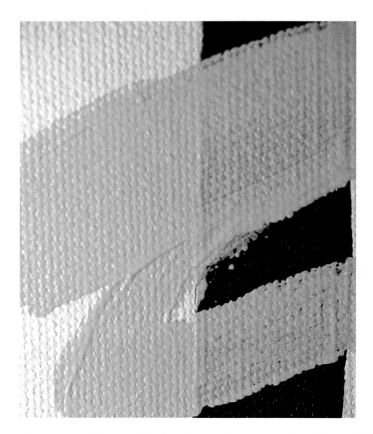

Two acrylic colors over black test bars: Genuine Cadmium Yellow (left) and Transparent Yellow (Azo). These two yellows embody the physical properties of the pigments used in their production: solid opacity for the cadmium, and jewel-like translucency for the Transparent Azo Yellow.

Titanium White mixed with Cadmium Red (left), and Mixing White (Winsor & Newton Finity Acrylic) with Cadmium Red (right). Titanium is the most opaque of the whites. Notice that the Titanium White mixture is more dense and chalky, and is dominated by the white. The mixture made with Mixing White allows the color to be tinted more gradually and without losing the brightness of the original red, because of the greater transparency of the white pigment. This sample is done with acrylic colors, but Zinc White is the comparable, more transparent white for mixing in oils.

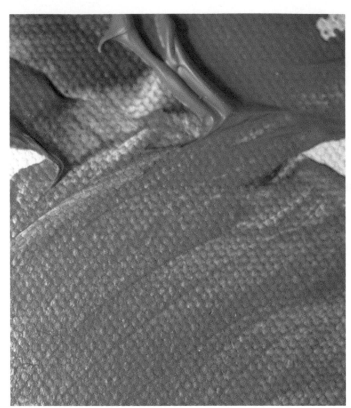

Yellow Ochre mixed with black (left) and Yellow Ochre mixed with Davy's gray (right). Davy's gray has historically been made from slate for oil colors, but is currently available with slightly different pigmentation in acrylics, as well. It's a transparent mixing color that has been traditionally used for tinting and graying down without overpowering the mixture.

By comparison, you can clearly see the granulation inherent in the Cobalt Blue swatch (right), compared to the neighboring, non-granulating Ultramarine. Courtesy of Winsor & Newton.

rather than to thicker, more viscous media. Some pigments, like cobalt and cerulean blue, have a tendency to agglomerate, or clump together slightly, leaving a mottled, granulated effect upon the surface. For many painters, granulation is highly desirable because it brings some unique textural character to the image (see the illustration immediately above). For

artists looking to minimize granulation, the use of distilled water will help.

Staining Colors

Again, this quality applies more to watercolor than to other media. Because watercolor relies upon the relative absorbency of the paper surface for stability, some colors that are made from very fine pigment will have a tendency to stain more than others. Staining isn't an issue until the painter tries to lift or sponge paint from the surface, only to find that the paper below has taken the color permanently. So, artists who commonly use lifting or scraping back (sgrafitto) techniques are well advised to know which of their paints are more likely to stain. The phthalocyanines and other modern synthetic pigments often produce staining colors.

The Modern Mystery: Traditional Versus Modern Colors

While I don't want to prejudice any readers about the nature of certain pigments, there are a few generalizations that can be of benefit, particularly when trying to make sense of the exploding variety of colors available. For example, the synthetic organic pigments (like the phthalocyanines, naphthols, pyrroles, arylides, and benzimidazolones), because of their small-particle, translucent, high-chroma nature, tend to be brighter, cleaner mixing, and tend toward staining more than their traditional inorganic brethren.

And, because we live in a world where reflected light and color combine into shadowed hues that are richly shaded with gray, the traditional, larger, rock-like, more opaque, inorganic pigments tend to mix in ways that more approximate the qualities of natural and shadowed light.

Now, it's not too terribly difficult to find examples in which each of these points will be proven wrong. There are traditional colors that offer high chroma, crystalline transparency, and bright mixes. And there are instances when synthetic organic colors can be the best choice for natural light images. (Note: Don't hesitate to add a touch of high-chroma organic color to a traditional mixture that has gone too dull and gray. It's a great way to add punch to a traditional color mix without sacrificing the traditional character.)

Nevertheless, these generalizations can help point the way to a better understanding of the choices available.

Reading the Labels and Literature

Now that you've read this far, and have built a substantial body of background information, there's a wealth of data available to you on the labels and within the color charts of conscientious manufacturers. In addition to the common name (such as "Alizarin Crimson" or "Fish Head Blue"), here's what you can expect to find on product labels:

• **Pigment content**, such as "cadmium sulfo-selenide" or "copper phthalocyanine." If the manufacturer desires to label the product in accordance with the ASTM standard D-4302, the pigment content will include the standardized Color Index name, such as PB (pigment blue) 29 for Ultramarine, or PY (pigment yellow) 40 for a potassium cobaltinitrite used in milling the color Aureolin.

• **Vehicle**, such as linseed oil, safflower oil, acrylic emulsion, gum Kordofan, or gum arabic.

• **Permanence ratings.** This can take a variety of forms. As you know, permanence is more than light-fastness, and the best manufacturers test and rate their colors for stability of the vehicle in addition, as well. Pay close attention to the ratings used by different manufacturers, for those should be based upon a

range of variables in addition to the ASTM lightfast-ness ratings of I (excellent) or II (very good).

• **Health label.** All colors are to include the ACMI (Art and Creative Materials Institute) health label and any required cautions, depending upon pigment or other content.

In addition to labeling upon the tube, there should be additional information available upon the color charts or within other forms of literature. For example, the literature may include indications of:

• **Transparency or opacity**
• **Granulation**
• **Staining**
• **Color Index number** as well as **Color Index name**
• **Further information about permanence.** For example, Winsor & Newton includes additional details, depending upon the pigment:

• "A" rated in full strength, may fade in thin washes (e.g. Aureolin).

• Cannot be relied upon to withstand damp (e.g. Cadmium Scarlet).

• Bleached by acids, acidic atmospheres (e.g. French Ultramarine).

And there's this interesting caveat:

• Fluctuating color; fades in light, recovers in dark (Prussian Blue).

Back to the fish heads. After asking a few questions of the gentleman in the broad cowboy hat, it didn't take long to figure out that he was looking for a method to save souvenirs from his favorite fishing excursions. We talked about a variety of options that could be employed, from very simple to exceedingly complicated. He decided upon a product that would allow him to simply stand the fish, headfirst, into a gel that would dry quickly to form a stable relief mold. Thankfully, he didn't have to worry about keeping the subject quiet and still, because no fish would ever consent to this process while alive. Once the fish was removed, he only had to pour plaster, and let it set to have a finished keepsake. The dried plaster could then be painted with any number color products.

After asking if the arrangement of heads was to be displayed indoors for the pleasure of family and friends, or outside, exposed to the elements, we were able to recommend a suitable varnish.

See? In this industry, there truly is something new to learn every day.

Chapter 5
Putting It Down:
Knowing and Using Your Medium

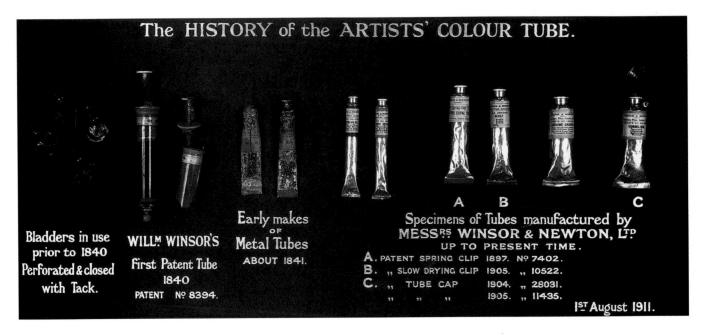

The paint syringe was first introduced in 1840, followed by the metal tube in 1841. Courtesy of Winsor & Newton.

A few years ago, I was asked to write a magazine article about ten products during the previous ten years that had changed the way we make art. I picked some things that were genuinely new to our community—new pigments like interference colors, new and better technology for making synthetic filament brushes, and alkyd painting mediums—and I also selected some things that were old but had become new again, like the explosion in handmade papers that we've seen over the last few years.

The piece wasn't intended to be taken too seriously, but it sure got me to thinking. I've talked and written for years about the direct relationship between the materials and how our art comes out. But writing that simple magazine article gave me the welcome and entertaining opportunity to look back over past generations and ask a single question: How would art be different without this or that product?

How many of us would be making art if the Fourdrinier paper-making machine had never been invented, and small amounts of paper, at very high cost, were available only to a very few individuals? Or what if nobody had thought of mixing pigment with linseed or safflower oils, creating a paint that allowed for dramatically more subtle and natural modeling?

What if there had never been tubes for paints, and we were still using pig bladders? Or we never had access to all of those new colors during the nineteenth century? Without either or both, you can make a pretty convincing argument that there never would have been an Impressionist movement, which wouldn't have led to the Fauvists or to Neo-Impressionism or to Expressionism or to… It goes on and on. And it points out a benchmark for anyone making art: the qualities of the tools shape the expressive image in profound ways.

There's no mistaking a virtuoso. Most painters develop a few signature strokes that set them apart, but Claude Monet was capable of virtually anything with a paintbrush. By the time Monet had painted "The Artist's Garden At Giverny," 1900, he had developed such range and skill that he could apply color to the surface with a degree of virtuosity that has seldom been matched before or since. Detail. Courtesy of Scala/Art Resource, NY.

A Word About Life and Learning to Paint

As we move into this chapter, now is a good time to make a general statement: Making art is hard work. There are magazines on the newsstand and maybe even in your mailbox that are filled with features like, "Four steps to great color," or "Five tips for realistic outdoor scenes." I know, because I've written some of them. And, there's value to each of those articles, because they can help identify some of the elements that lead to successful image making.

But the fact remains that you don't learn to paint in three or four or five steps. It's a process that takes time and untold dedication. Sometimes we make paintings that feel great, and that show real progress, and there are other times that it's a painful, Herculean struggle. But it's the combination of both the successes and the challenges that make it the pursuit worthwhile. It's the process that enriches and rewards. And in this era of have-it-now, instant gratification, there's nothing like painting or making art to help us remember that the most rewarding portions of our lives don't come in a cereal box or via overnight express. The richness in our lives, like good painting, is built layer by layer.

So, as you move forward in this book, and you see what may at first appear to be a daunting list of "rules of thumb" for using paint, or some chemical descriptions that seem confusing, give yourself time to absorb the concepts. It will all come together if you allow yourself the opportunity. And the pleasures can be exquisite.

Developing Your Skills

Before we jump into the specifics of using different media, I need to get something off my chest: There is a wide variety of sources, books, web sites, and videos that provides wonderful information about different techniques and applications. And, because some may feel this book is overlong as is, I won't presume to duplicate information you can get elsewhere. For a partial list of resources that offer great instruction and techniques, consult Chapter 8.

The first four chapters of the book have been devoted to history, how color is made, and the essential characteristics of pigment and paint. This chapter is about something more direct: how you put the color on the surface...

Watercolor

Some consider it the most demanding of all media. It's certainly the most "Zen." Because you can't scrape off what didn't work yesterday—like you can with oils—or fully obliterate a less-than-successful section and start over—as you can with acrylics—watercolor doesn't offer much in the way of second chances. It demands great immediacy. All of your skill, experience, focus, heart, and soul must be in your fingers as you move toward the paper. And there are times when you have to say, "I have no idea what's going to happen when I lay this color down in a wash, but I'm just going to have to have faith that the color knows the way."

I love watercolor. As much as I enjoy the mechanics and the techniques of oil, acrylic, and other media, watercolor is where I found my painting home. So, bear with me if I wax poetic.

The magic of watercolor comes from a variety of sources, including the nature of the pigment and the clarity and solubility of the gum. But, more than anything, the character of the color comes from something absolutely magical and miraculous. Something that we take very much for granted.

When my son Christopher was about a year-and-a-half old, and trying really hard to make use of words, he was constantly on the lookout for water. Everywhere we went, he'd wave wildly at streams, rivers, ponds, swimming pools, puddles in the gutter, and sprinklers. He'd get so excited that he'd begin to shake and quiver, hollering, "Wadda, Daddee! Wadda!" At first it was amusing, and then, as so often happens when my kids do something surprising, I started to wonder if there was more to this. I started trying to see the water through his little-boy eyes. And the magic became immediately obvious.

Water is astonishing. It moves, flows, and changes shape in miraculous ways. It sparkles and shimmers, reflecting not only light, but a shifting, reversed image of the world around us. It feels wonderful in our hands or as it moves across our bodies. No wonder Christopher got so excited. I'm sure it seemed to him like the most amazing thing he'd ever seen. And I got excited too, seeing fresh magic in something that, before my child had awakened me, had seemed so common.

The nature of watercolor can be found in the nature of water, for the paint, too, moves and flows in miraculous ways. Here's why:

"Nine Maidens Circle, Penrith," by Emma Pearce, 14 x 10 inches. The nature of watercolor makes it particularly well-suited for the creation of gleaming, radiant images.

"Tree," watercolor, by the author, 1991. Watercolor often has a mind of its own, and sometimes just needs to be turned loose.

Noon Tucson   DPyle '44

Two watercolors: "Noon, Tucson" and "Dusk, Tucson," by the author. The process of making art is a long one, requiring patience, dedication, and repeated attempts. Sometimes it helps to revisit the same subject under different conditions.

Dusk Tucson

"Pont Neuf Bridge," watercolor on handmade paper, by the author. Ever since my son instructed me on the magic of water, I've been fascinated by its ever-shifting surface as a painting subject. Notice how the toned paper and ground help unify the painting.

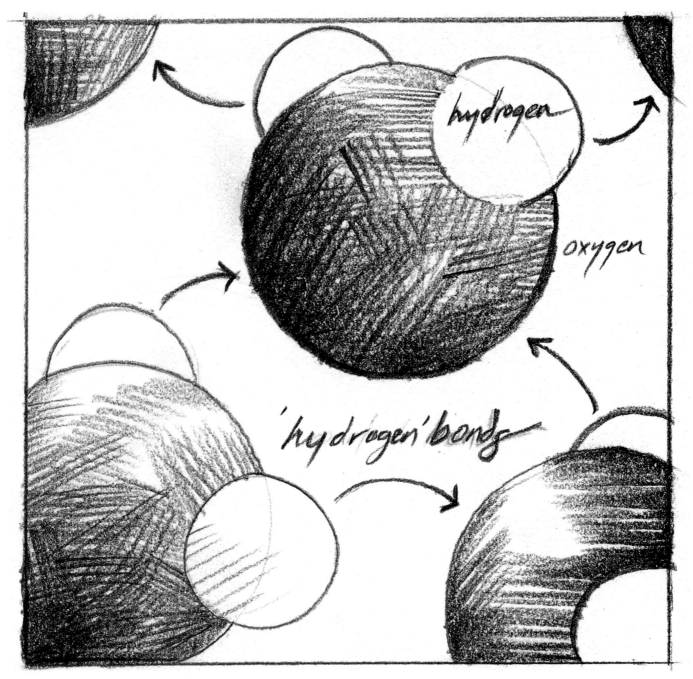

Water molecules, in the shape of the head of an internationally famous mouse, are loosely attached to one another through a phenomenon called "hydrogen bonding."

Ears in the Water

Water acts like water by virtue of something called "hydrogen bonding." (I always remember that name by thinking of a handsome, tuxedoed secret agent who, after being asked his name, replies, "Bond. Hydrogen Bond.")

To understand hydrogen bonding, think of water as being made up of gazillions of tiny Mickey Mouse heads. Those are water molecules, and each Mickey-face is an oxygen, while the Mickey-ears are hydro-gens (H_2O, of course, is the real-life appellation). Because (for reasons that we won't go into here) the electrical energy within every water molecule is distributed a bit unevenly, the Mickey-ear-hydrogens are attracted to Mickey-face-oxygens on neighboring molecules. And because of this molecule-to-molecule attraction, all of the Mickey-water-molecules are loosely attached—or "hydrogen bonded"—to each other.

This bond is what makes water so incredibly cool. When water is dropped, it pulls itself into a

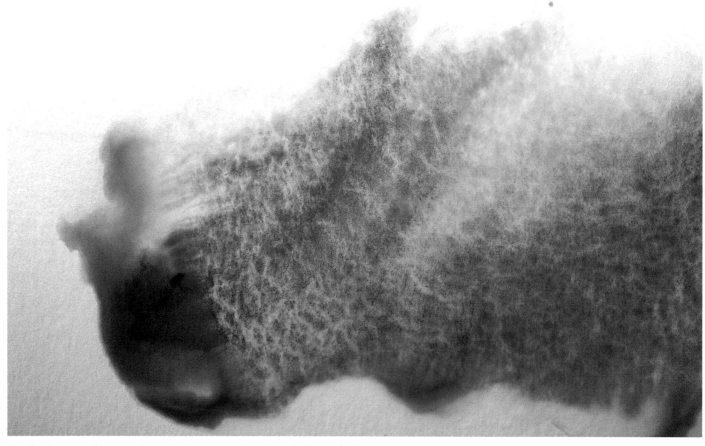

The fluid nature of watercolor is both its strength and its challenge for the artist.

ball. Hydrogen bonding. When water freezes, it lines up into a crystal lattice structure. Hydrogen bonding. Lightweight bugs run across the surface of liquid water, and don't fall through. Hydrogen bonding. You do a belly-flop and DO break through, and it really hurts because you have to force past the surface tension of the water. Hydrogen bonding. When you load your fine Kolinsky sable brush with color, the water pulls itself, and the brush hairs along with it, into a rapier-like point. Hydrogen bonding. And when you spread that color upon the paper, the mixture of gum and water flows, moves, and shimmies across the paper surface because of—what else?—the hydrogen bonding.

If that's not magic, then I don't know what is.

Where It Comes From

Of all paint, watercolor has the longest history. Remember our Cro-Magnon guy, inadvertently mixing earth pigment with the bear fat and saliva in his mouth? That was the first watercolor.

Over the course of a few millennia, and by a number of different cultures, it was discovered that other vehicles could be mixed with water and used

with pigment as paint. As early as the twelfth century, there are written accounts of tree gums being used as a paint vehicle, and they may, in fact, have been used long before.

Mssrs. William Winsor and Henry Newton of London were the first to produce a modern water-color with a gum arabic vehicle that remained easily soluble under a variety of conditions. Winsor & Newton built their company (launched in 1832) first on moist watercolors, then on other media. Then came the paint tube, also first brought to market and patented by Winsor & Newton, allowing watercolor to be transported and used virtually anytime, anywhere.

The Gum Vehicle and What It Does

Modern watercolors are milled upon a triple-roll mill, into a finely balanced suspension. Because of its stability and even solubility, gum arabic is the vehicle of choice. When well-milled, just as with oil colors, watercolors shouldn't separate within the tube and will remain perfectly usable for years.

If you thought that a gum is a gum, then chew on this: gum arabic comes from the acacia tree. And not

Natural gums. Courtesy of Winsor & Newton.

just any old acacia tree, but from acacia trees in Africa. And not just any old place Africa, but from acacia trees in the relatively small regions of Senegal or the Sudan. And what, you may ask, is so special about this particular gum? Why are other gums from other acacia trees just watercolor wannabes?

Gum Kordofan or gum Senegal (the proper names for this specific gum) dissolve in water with no residue. In solution with water, they are absolutely clear and highly stable. Other gums just can't compare in stability or in clarity.

Whether for watercolor, oil, acrylic, egg tempera, or encaustic, the function of a vehicle is to do the following:

• **Coat and carry the pigment.** The pigment must be evenly dispersed, and stay that way indefinitely.

• **Be optically clear.** A vehicle that is colorless, or at least very pale in color, is essential. When milling watercolor, if a gum with dark color is used, some of the natural character of the pigment will be altered and compromised.

• **Form a permanent, stable film.** As mentioned in Chapter 3, the stable color surface is formed differently with watercolor than with the intact films formed by oil or acrylic vehicles. The gum vehicle facilitates an even solution with water, allowing the color to spread evenly and to settle into the slightly absorbent topmost portion of the paper. Ultimately, the stability of the color comes from the combined forces of the gum film held within the structure of the paper surface.

• **Bring favorable working properties to the paint.** Fine gum allows for even solution, flow, and control over the color.

In addition to the above properties, the vehicle for watercolor has another seemingly conflicting task. When used straight from the tube or pan, we watercolor-types want the color to be immediately soluble. We want the paint to take on water like a camel after a month in the Sahara, and then flow across the paper surface in a river of expressive glee. Yet, once the color has set, and we're ready to apply the next layer or wash, we want that first layer to, all of a sudden, reverse its nature and stay put, remaining fully INsoluble under the new, sluicing wash of color above. Heaven forbid that the new wash should redissolve the first, leaving the painter with nothing but costly mud upon the surface. Talk about wanting to have your cake and eat it too!

Yet, well-made watercolor, milled with generations of expertise and with the best available gum Kordofan or gum Senegal, will do exactly that. And that's one of the characteristics of truly fine watercolors: not only do you get brilliant colors, single pigment characteristics, and even dispersion and flow, but you also get a paint that magically shifts its nature, going from willing solubility right out of the tube or pan, to stable insolubility, allowing you to build glowing, jewel-like layers of color.

All in the Family: Transparent Watercolors and Gouache

There are two members of the watercolor family. The first, **transparent watercolor**, is most commonly used by fine artists. The color is not wholly transparent; it merely has a greater tendency in that direction. The paint is most commonly used to take advantage of that transparent quality, allowing the color of the surface below (usually, but not always, white paper) to show through, bringing a characteristic radiance to the image. The transparency varies, with some colors like the cadmiums being quite opaque, and others being distinctly translucent. As always, with well-made color, the quality of transparency to opacity is a function of the pigment's physical properties.

Other additives are commonly included in the formulation of watercolors to enhance solubility, to retain moisture, and to manage the flow and working characteristics. These can include starches like dextrin and humectants like glycerine. Some manufacturers promote the fact that they use honey, and while there's undeniable romance in honey over something more chemical-sounding, like dextrin, honey can darken with age and doesn't appear to be as stable as other additives.

Gouache, or opaque watercolor, is the second member of the family. Gum arabic serves as the vehicle, just like with transparent watercolor, but there are other things done to the color to make it opaque. Gouache is commonly used in more commercial applications, where dense, flat color is an advantage. Over the past few years, however, there has been some renewed interest by fine artists in using gouache as an expressive medium on its own merits. Here are the benchmarks generally considered to contribute to the ideal gouache:

• **Dense, opaque color.** There's two ways to get

opaque color: either you add an opacifier, like chalk or calcium carbonate, or you pack the formulation with so much pigment that the density and opacity happen without compromising the true pigment qualities. The majority of manufacturers do the former. Only a tiny few, that I know of, do the latter.

• **Purity of color.** This becomes problematic with gouache. Because so many manufacturers use opacifiers to gain opacity and workability, the color purity is often compromised. This also, however, helps the very best products emerge clearly from the rest of the field.

Why Be So Wishy-washy? What's the Best?

During the course of writing this book, I have gone to great pains to fairly represent the benchmarks that make great color, hoping to educate you, dear reader, in such a way that you'll be confident in choosing the manufacturer and product that you think best meet your individual needs. Because there are a number of fine, dedicated producers of color that comprise this industry, I've chosen to not make any overt endorsements, hoping to represent the community as a whole, rather than a single manufacturer. At the same time, I make no secret of my long affiliation Winsor & Newton, an association that comes by happy choice, for I simply couldn't represent a brand of color that didn't come from people of integrity, or of unrepentant dedication to making the finest color possible within each of the targeted user, or quality, categories.

The reason I say this now is because I'm about to make a categorical endorsement. In oil, acrylic, and transparent watercolor, I have strong personal favorites, but those are better disclosed informally, over a cup of coffee. In the world of gouache, however, there is a clear standard, not approached by any other product that I know. Winsor & Newton Designer's Gouache is a remarkable range of colors. Because of standards developed over centuries by the company, unparalleled resources, and skill, Winsor & Newton has been able to produce a product that dominates its category. The opacity of the color comes exclusively from the pigment load, not from any added opacifiers. The colors, therefore, are remarkably pure. The color dries to a flat, evenly matte surface, is easily and evenly workable, and levels out upon drying. It is expensive, but, as with any truly fine color, is worth every single penny.

Gouache differs from transparent watercolor in its opacity, its matte surface when dry, and its leveling properties.

- **Even brushability.** The color should be evenly and easily applied, and it should produce a...
- **...self-leveling surface upon drying.**

A word of caution for fine artists using gouache: Because gouache has been produced primarily for commercial applications, where the work is photographed and then filed, and long-term permanence is not an issue, most ranges of opaque watercolor include a significant number of non-lightfast colors. Bottom line? Pay attention to the permanence ratings upon the labels and choose accordingly.

Shifting Color

Water bends and refracts light differently than pigment, than gum, and than any of the vehicles used in making color. For that reason, there's an ever-present need to manage, or at least be aware of the color shift that occurs as water goes into, or evaporates out of, your color mix. With watercolor, colors often tend to lose much of their brilliance once the color has dried. While you never entirely eliminate a color shift, you can minimize it. How? Buy the best quality color you can afford. The good stuff maintains its brilliance, wet or dry.

Pigment Character

As with any medium, the character of the pigments used in watercolor finds unique ways in which to assert itself.

Transparency and opacity. With transparent watercolor, in particular, you'll find yourself able to take advantage of the natural opacity or transparency of individual pigments. The colors that are supposed to be opaque, like the cadmiums, offer good coverage. And the ones that are naturally transparent take on an almost transcendent, illuminative quality.

Granulating. Some mineral pigments, like the cobalts or the natural earths, are characterized by a large particle size. And as the color settles, the particles make for a granular effect. Some artists look for granulating colors, feeling that the natural texture brings a unique character to the image. If desired, granulation can be minimized (although never wholly eliminated) by using distilled water.

Flocculating pigments create a visual effect that is similar to granulating colors, although through a slightly different mechanism. Flocculating colors are made from pigments that, upon settling on the paper surface, like to "hang together," leaving a mottled effect.

Staining. Many of the modern organic colors, like the phthalocyanines, are of such small particle size, and of such great tinting strength, that they tend to stain the paper. The practical implication is that you may well find it impossible to go back and sponge or lift a still-wet layer.

Building the Perfect Watercolor Painting

While I don't want to minimize the importance of careful technique, the fact remains that, when working in watercolor, if you choose the best quality materials, and lightfast colors, you're likely to end up with a stable image. It's not like using oils, where great attention must be paid to the careful application and deliberate construction of a stable film.

Let's start with the surface. A complete, unabashedly romantic and passionate discussion of paper is

being saved for a later publication. Even so, it's important to offer a few tidbits to help you in choosing from the myriad of watercolor papers on the market. Here are:

Seven Paper Terms Everyone Should Know

Hot press is the term used to describe many papers that have a very smooth surface. The term is, in fact, a misnomer because there's no heat involved: the newly formed and dried sheet is fed through "calender" rollers that smooth the surface to a fine, even texture. Hot press is ideal for doing fine detail work in watercolor or pen and ink.

Cold press papers have a moderate degree of tooth. They're suitable for watercolor and drawing with some detail. The surface texture adds a bit of flair and character.

Rough. The dramatic texture of rough-surfaced paper can make for a remarkable painting and drawing experience. Here's where the paper's voice speaks loudest and with greatest force. While not suitable for fine detail, the results can be startling on rough paper if the artist works in a broad or spontaneous manner and craves a dynamic surface.

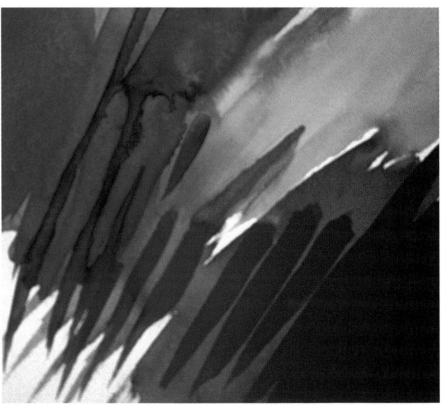

The character of the surface can make a dramatic difference in the character of the color and the image. The color on the left has been applied to a smooth, hot press paper surface, while the color on the right is on a rough surface.

Formation. When the sheet is formed it will take an impression from the screen. "Wove" formation is the most common and results from a screen that resembles window screening. The less common "laid" formation is the impression from a screen made of narrow metal strips that have been stitched together at 1- to 2-inch intervals. The result is a distinctive "laid and chain" pattern.

Watching your weights... Why is 140lb watercolor paper called 140lb? When the weight of a paper is listed in pounds, a specific number of those sheets (usually 500), in a specific size will weigh a certain amount. Or, 500 sheets of 140lb watercolor paper, in size 22" x 30," weighs 140 pounds. Easy, right? Wrong. This gets confusing when comparing sheets of different sizes. A 300lb watercolor paper is about the same "weight" or thickness as one that is listed as 1114lb. The difference is that the 300lb paper uses a basis size of 22" x 30" and the 1114lb uses a basis size of 40" x 60." Oh my.

More and more papers are being labeled with "grams per square meter." In this system, the 300lb and the 1114lb are both specified to have a weight of 640 g/m2. This means that a square meter of this paper will weigh, by itself, 640 grams. This system eliminates the confusion resulting from trying to keep track of those pesky different sheet sizes.

Sizing. To control paper absorbency, "sizing" is added. If the sizing agent is added in the vat when the pulp is prepared, it's called "internal" sizing. If it's added to the surface of the formed sheet, it's called "tub" or surface sizing. Traditional watercolor papers are surface sized to control the water or paint absorbency as much as possible. Papers with no sizing at all are called "waterleaf."

Acid-free or pH neutral. These terms are not interchangeable. Acid is the evil enemy of paper—it's what makes paper yellow and crumble. Paper that is measured to have a perfect balance of acid to its alkaline counterpart has a pH measurement of 7.0 (or very close) and is pH neutral. Paper that is measured to have a greater ratio of alkaline to acid (with no acid roaming about to pillage poor, unsuspecting paper fibers) has a pH ranging from 6.5 to 8.5 and is called "acid free."

Note: Neutrality can be considered an indicator of permanence, but it's no guarantee.

And Then Ten More Things to Know About Painting Upon Paper...

Tooth describes the surface landscape; the lumps and bumps, the hills and valleys. Tooth adds character and it's also essential for good adhesion when using pastel, charcoal, or graphite.

The **watermark** is an impression left in the paper by a wire sewn to the papermaking screen. It's used to indicate the mill. Some watermarks can be beautiful!

A **deckle edge** refers to the uneven edge of the paper. A natural deckle edge is the result of pulp that seeps between the screen and the deckle (a frame placed over the screen during paper formation). Mechanical deckles are produced on some papers.

Thick or thin? The thickness of the paper is particularly important when working in watercolor. The thicker the sheet, the less it will curl and buckle (generally speaking) as it becomes wet. A thinner sheet can be fine for drawing.

How far can you go with the deckle? Twinrocker, a mill in Brookston, Indiana, that produces only handmade papers, offers many of its sheets with a "feather" deckle. The painting appears as if its floating upon a cloud.

Absorbency. How much color the paper will absorb is critical for watercolorists and printmakers. For drawing, it's not much of an issue. A fine watercolor paper will absorb just the right amount of media so the color will "set" upon the surface. This means the color will remain brilliant and won't "feather" out from the original brush stroke. Printmaking papers need to be a bit more absorbent to pull the image or ink from printing plate.

Will it take a licking? Durability is the issue here. Some papers will take erasing, scrubbing, and sponging all day long, and the surface just keeps going and going and going. Other papers, because of a softer surface, just don't hold up under repeated attacks—using an eraser or scrubbing with your brush may pull the surface right up. You can often (but not always) tell the durable from the fragile by touch and feel: a soft-surfaced sheet is usually less likely to take hard-hitting abuse.

Stretching. When wet, some papers will buckle and roll like a drunken abstract expressionist. Generally, if the paper is thicker or greater in weight than 200lb, it's not necessary to stretch. If the artist is working on a lighter sheet, however, stretching will keep it perfectly flat, even when sopping wet.

Stretching is simple, even though it does take planning to allow the paper to dry before painting. There are products on the market specifically intended for stretching, or you can use a stapler and a sturdy board that won't warp. Soak the paper thoroughly (what did you think your bathtub was for?) and then staple along the edges to the mounting surface. Keep the paper as flat as possible. Two-inch gummed tape (the kind you have to moisten) will also work nicely. As the paper dries, you'll have a perfectly flat, drum-tight surface to work upon. When the painting is done, simply remove the staples or use a utility knife to carefully trim the paper away from the tape.

Do I always have to work on a white sheet? Heavens, no! A toned or colored paper means a consistent hue running through the image. It's a dandy way to unify a painting or drawing from the very outset. Because the luminous quality of watercolor depends upon light reflected through the paint from the paper surface below, a toned ground adds a uniform cast to the painting's highlights.

Wet and dry effects. For detail or precise work, a dry sheet is best. Adding color to a surface that is already moist means the colors will mingle with unpredictable and, often, highly atmospheric results.

Can I only use watercolor paper for watercolor? There are no paper police on patrol—don't be afraid to experiment! There are many soft, absorbent oriental sheets, such as Hosho or Kochi (*Gesundheit!*), that offer delightful effects with watercolor. Watercolor and printmaking papers can be terrific for drawing.

And, Finally, One Really Critical Thing to Understand About Paper Permanence...

The most permanent papers are made from fibers that are durable to begin with. Plant fibers that are long, strong, and resilient make great paper. Many fibers will resist degradation even if they do become slightly acidic. In western papermaking, the most common durable fibers are cotton and flax (linen). Eastern papermakers commonly use durable fibers such as kozo, mitsumata, or gampi.

Quite simply, if the paper is responsibly made, with a minimum of foreign additives and made from a strong durable fiber, you'll have a durable sheet.

The Medium Scoop: What Do They Do, and When Can I Use Mediums?

Watercolor is typically used in such a "raw" state that hardly anybody ever adds anything to the color. But there are mediums that can be added to alter the performance and character of the color. Here's a rundown on the most common:

Traditional Mediums

Gum arabic can be used as an additive medium to do all kinds of nice things with watercolor. Adding a little gum to your mix will boost the brilliance of the color and will mitigate the color shift as water evaporates from the mix.

Ox Gall. Remember our discussion about the nature of water and the magic of bond, hydrogen bond? Ox Gall acts to interfere with, or loosen, the hydrogen bond from one Mickey-water-molecule to the next. It loosens up the water, allowing it to spread more easily and making it "wetter." Ox Gall is a wonderful medium when you want to improve the flow of watercolor. The color becomes more fluid and spreads more rapidly. It's also terrific when working wet-into-wet, making for dramatic spreading of one color into another. And it can lessen the effect commonly known as "blooming" as a particularly wet area of color dries.

Mediums that change the working character can be added to watercolor, just like oils and acrylics.

Non-traditional Mediums

Winsor & Newton has recently introduced six mediums for use with watercolor. "There's been great excitement with the introduction of our new mediums," says Emma Pearce, Technical Services Manager for Winsor & Newton in Wealdstone, England. "And we're expecting more from them over the next few years. Just like when an artist adds new colors to his or her palette, you don't try six at once; you go one at a time, and it takes you a couple of years to learn how to make use of these new opportunities."

The new mediums are:
• Granulation medium (for bringing a mottled appearance to the color)
• Blending medium (for slowing drying and easier blending)
• Lifting preparation (to allow for easier lifting or sponging of colors from the surface)
• Permanent masking medium (for isolating areas of detail)
• Texture medium
• Iridescent medium

The Brush for Watercolor

This is a book about paints and colors. But you can't use paint without some implement for application. So, even though I'm saving much of the detail for a later publication, it would be irresponsible to not include some basic information about choosing the right brush for use with watercolors. Here goes:

Every watercolor brush in the world does three important things; it's how well these things are done that separates the real brushes from the sticks with tied-on hair. Here are the three benchmarks that every watercolor brush aspires to:

• **A great point or edge.** Without a fine, dependable point, how are you to place the color exactly right?
• **Perfect "snap" or spring.** When you lift a brush from the painting surface, it should snap right back into shape.
• **Even flow control.** This is most important of all. The brush should dispense color consistently and predictably.

Here are the common hairs and filaments used for watercolor brushes:

Brushes dating to 1865. Courtesy of Winsor & Newton.

Fine brushmaking is an art by itself. While much of the brushmaking process has been automated, the very best brushes are still made one-by-one, with great skill and care, by hand. Courtesy of Winsor & Newton.

The Kolinsky Pinnacle

The brush hair that measures up best is Kolinsky sable. These little beasties are members of the marten, or mink, family and are native to Siberia, China, and Korea, where the winters are brutally cold.

Kolinsky hairs are conical in shape, with a "belly" in the middle that tapers to a breathtaking point. The terms "snap" and "spring" were invented just for this hair. And Kolinsky hairs are ringed with irregularities or scales that make for even, dependable color flow when the loaded brush is laid upon the surface. Color comes off the point for what seems like days and with stunning consistency.

There are different grades of Kolinsky, but the very best come from Siberia, where our planet gets deeply serious about cold. The hairs are taken from

the top of the male's tail (where they're longest and in the best condition) during the deepest, dead of winter. The animals don't fare well in captivity, so the hair comes only from wild Kolinskies.

With those conditions, you can see why first-quality Kolinsky, ounce for ounce, is more costly than gold. The finest Kolinsky is a soft, golden-brown color that darkens at the tip. Hairs from other parts of the sable pelt are used in lesser quality brushes. Second-quality hairs are shorter and distinctly less "springy" than their top-notch counterparts. How do you know the difference?

There's no substitute for taking a brush for a test drive. The point, snap, and flow control of a truly fine brush will be obvious. It will make you quiver, speak in tongues, and never want to be without it.

Second-best Sable

Hair from the tail of the weasel is commonly used for making low- to medium-priced "red sable" or "sable" brushes. Weasel hair doesn't offer the same sterling qualities of honest-to-goodness Kolinsky, but it's still quite good and significantly less costly. Weasel hair is usually red to reddish-brown.

Squirrel

Top-grade squirrel hair comes from Russia and features a rapier point (like Kolinsky) and excellent flow control (also like Kolinsky) but little spring (NOT like Kolinsky). Squirrel is used for making mop or wash brushes.

The very best Russian squirrel is used for making large, wonderful watercolor brushes notable for the brass or copper-wrapped, goose-quill ferrule. These brushes (called *Petit Gris* by the French) are exceedingly versatile and economical when compared to sable, and very popular in Europe. They are, however, not as well suited for glazing, or building one layer of color over another. The hair is rougher than that of sable and can abrade a color layer, lifting dried paint from an earlier application and mixing it with the newly applied color. Storing huge volumes of color, they dispense great, flowing washes. And they hold a terrific point.

Oh Sabeline! Won't You Be True?

Sabeline is imitation sable and comes, in fact, from the ox. Yes, the ox! Even though the two animals are not often mistaken for each other, ox hair can be bleached and then dyed to roughly resemble sable. Sabeline offers reasonable flow control but not much spring and a point like your elbow.

Camel Hair

How many camels does it take to make a camel-hair brush? None. The camel brush is the art material equivalent of a tossed salad—it's usually a mix of ox, pony, and bargain-basement squirrel. Some camel brushes hold a good load of watercolor (hence the name camel (?) but have no point or spring.

The Synthetic Revolution

When nylon fiber was invented, it made perfect sense to adapt it to making artists' brushes. The advantage? Low price. The disadvantage? Less than great performance.

Nylon originally came equipped with no point. It offered too much spring, making the brush difficult to control. Worst of all, when the filament is extruded, it's smooth as glass. No capillary action. No flow control over fluid paints. Early synthetic brushes were like paint dump trucks, spewing color uncontrollably across the surface.

But things have changed. New and improved nylon, as well as another miracle fiber, polyester, has come to our rescue. In addition to being perfect for leisure suits and bad ties, newer nylon and polyesters can be produced with a point. And, best of all, the filaments can be bundled in different diameters to manage spring, as well as to better carry and control the color. The result? Precious flow control!

Within the last few years, newer synthetic filament (most commonly called "golden nylon" or "taklon") brushes have hit the market, offering outstanding performance at very reasonable cost. They still can't quite keep up with a fine sable or Kolinsky. But, for the first time, beginners can afford to hop aboard the watercolor train with a brush that will assist rather than hinder.

Synthetic brushes are also more durable under certain conditions. Bugs and moths certainly find them less tasty than natural hair.

In years past, how many novice watercolorists have simply given up when, unknown to them, it was a brutish brush that was blocking success rather than skill or ability? No more. The arrival of good synthetic brushes at affordable prices qualifies as a truly big deal!

Tips on Framing

There's one, all-important tip when it comes to determining when and how to frame watercolors under glass: Do it.

Because of the greater fragility of the color and paper (when compared to the stable films of oil or acrylics), it's essential that any displayed image be presented and preserved under glass, rather than exposed to the atmosphere.

Beyond that, here are a couple of suggestions regarding framing:
• If permanence is your aim, always mat with or mount upon museum board or some other museum-quality matt board. Beware of the manufacturers that promote their lowest cost boards as acid-free. The term has become a bit of a buzzword in recent years, and, while low-cost board may indeed be

Watercolors on display require framing for protection.

Oil Color

So, what's the big deal with oil colors? Why are they so popular, even after five hundred years, and after plenty of other new mediums and pretenders to the throne of canvas or panel painting have arrived on the scene? Because there's still nothing quite like glorious, brilliant color that comes with fine oils.

Now that you understand the constituents of oil color, and how they're milled into paint, you can also understand what makes them so unique: in finely milled oil color, each particle of pigment is surrounded, enveloped, and embraced by a perfect layer of oil. And it's that layer of oil that gives the color the unique optical properties that keep artists coming back. As light moves through the layer of paint, it dances and cavorts through the oil, bringing a shimmering depth and richness to the color that can't be matched by any other medium.

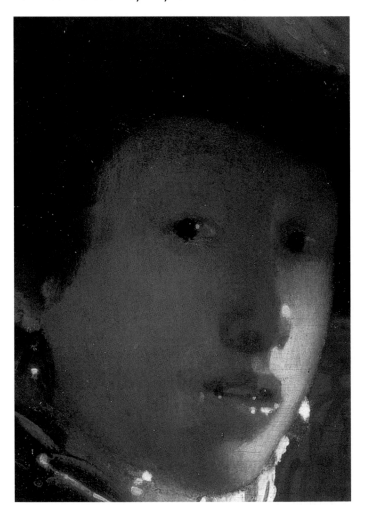

Detail. "Girl with the Red Hat," by Johannes Vermeer, 1665–66, oil on panel. Photograph Board of Trustees, National Gallery of Art, Washington. Andrew W. Mellon Collection.

acid-free when it leaves the mill, it may not stay that way for long. Museum boards, as well as boards made from rag, or pure, "alpha" pulp, are produced to be acid-free and stable for the long term. Also, use only museum-quality adhesives or mounting corners.
• Always mount your work with spacers or behind a matte to ensure that the image surface never comes in contact with the glass.

And oils have, with careful milling and proper application by the artist, proven that they can stand the test of time. As discussed in the previous chapter (Be Like Van Eyck!), there are paintings done with oil that have passed the five-hundred year mark with smooth, stable surfaces.

Before looking at the step-by-step application of oils, we should briefly discuss...

...The Oil Vehicle and What It Does

As stated before, the vehicle for any color—whether it's oil, acrylic, watercolor, encaustic, or any other paint—should do the following:
- Coat and carry the pigment,
- Form a permanent, stable film, and
- Bring favorable working properties to the paint.

There are a variety of different vegetable oils that meet those criteria, the most popular of which is linseed oil from the flax plant. Linseed oil is clear, stable, and slightly yellow, and it will carry a high load of pigment in a finely balanced suspension. When milled properly, it dries evenly and makes for a highly workable and brushable paint body. There's no denying the tactile and frankly sensual quality of laying fine color upon painting surface.

A few manufacturers, because of slightly different working properties, choose walnut oil as a vehicle. While walnut oil brings some unique properties to the color, it can have a tendency to darken more than linseed oil, and there is some contention that it has a greater tendency to go rancid.

Safflower oil is a semi-drying oil, meaning that it dries slower than linseed oil. Because it's lighter in color and less prone to yellowing, safflower oil is used in milling whites by some manufacturers.

As mentioned in Chapter 4, semi-drying oils, like safflower and poppy seed, raise some interesting chemical issues. They're perfectly suitable for general use, and they mix exceedingly well with linseed oil-based colors. But, because they expand and contract

Different drying oils have different color and characteristics. Each will coat and carry the pigment in unique ways. Courtesy of Winsor & Newton.

during drying at a different rate than linseed oil colors, they should not be used for underpainting or as a ground. An Underpainting White or Foundation White in linseed oil should be used for that purpose. And the different expansion and contraction rates don't appreciably affect colors mixed with safflower based whites, as long as the rule of fat over lean—or flexible over less flexible—is observed. More on that in just a few pages.

All in the Family: The Different Kinds of Oil Color

In simple terms, oil color is made of pigment evenly dispersed in vegetable oil. Beyond that simple definition, however, there are a surprising number of choices available: traditional colors in linseed oil or safflower oil, alkyd-based oil colors, paint bars, and, now, oils that mix with water. Here are the qualities that you can expect from each:

Conventional or Traditional Oils

Traditional oils are milled with a drying oil (usually linseed). Artists' grade oil colors carry a high load of pigment. The colors dry to the touch in approximately two to twelve days (depending upon color). They reach a stable state of dryness, and are ready for varnishing, in about six months (longer for thick films of color). With proper technique and application, paintings created from traditional oils can last for centuries.

Alkyd-based Oil Colors

Alkyds are relative newcomers to the oil color fray. The vehicle is made from a natural oil (usually soy-based, in the art materials industry) that undergoes some laboratory transmogrification to make it faster drying and suitable for use as a color vehicle. The oil is polymerized (Remember that term? Polymers are long molecular chains that are made up of identical or nearly identical smaller building blocks. The small blocks that link up are called "monomers.") in a reaction with an alcohol and an acid; hence, the name. Alcohol-acid… alc-id… alkyd! The resulting substance is resin-like and is put into solution with a mild mineral spirit solvent to work as a medium or vehicle with pigment.

Alkyds bring some different qualities to the palette. They work much like traditional oils and require solvents for thinning, but they dry much more rapidly. The colors remain workable for four to six hours. They become touch-dry in eighteen to twenty-four hours and are ready for varnishing in about a month (longer with thick color films).

The physical properties of alkyd prevent them from carrying quite as much pigment in dispersion as linseed oil colors. The result is a color of slightly greater transparency. While alkyds don't offer quite the same level of opacity with naturally opaque pigments, many artists have decided that—because of the rapid drying and the tendency toward transparency—they are superior for painting styles that depend upon lots of glazes and layering. And, as long as the rules of fat over lean, or flexible over less flexible, are observed, alkyd colors can be used in combination with traditional oils.

At the time of this writing, the only true alkyd-based oil colors are the Griffin Fast-drying Oils from Winsor & Newton. Other manufacturers have opted for using alkyd resins as the basis for additive mediums rather than an entire range of color. More on those later in this chapter.

Alkyds and other newer mediums raise some interesting questions about permanence and stability. We know that well-milled oil color will stand the test of time. We know the same about fine watercolor. But vehicles and media that have been around for only a decade or two or five don't yet have that track record. Determining the long-term stability of a relatively new color and vehicle requires accelerated aging tests, as well as some pretty careful chemistry. Even then, the absolutely, positively final word on permanence won't be known for a couple of centuries.

That said, there's every reason to believe that alkyds, acrylics, and now some of the new water-mixable oils should be highly stable (as long as they're applied with the appropriate technique). The drying mechanism of alkyds, and the finished polymeric structure of the film, give every indication that the color should be stable indefinitely. In fact, Dr. Marion Mecklenburg, a Senior Research Chemist with the Smithsonian in Washington, DC, has found that alkyd films, after a number of years of testing, are proving to be significantly more flexible than films made with traditional oils. And greater flexibility and elasticity is an excellent indicator of greater resistance to shock or stress, and, quite likely, of long-term stability.

Now that we've seen a few generations of acrylic emulsion come and go, the same can be said

Paint bars are oil colors stiffened with wax. They're direct, juicy, and great fun!

Water-mixable oils work like traditional oil color. The only practical difference is that water serves as a solvent, rather than turpentine or mineral spirits. There are even water-mixable oil additive mediums available.

of acrylics. And, as we'll see in a section on page 109, the same can be said—with a qualifier or two—of water-mixable oils.

Paint Bars

For centuries, waxes have been used to bring increased stiffness to oil color. Waxes mix readily with linseed oil, and they remain stable within the final film. Adding some wax makes a stiff color. Add more wax, and you get a stick of paint.

Paint bars are great fun. They're immediate and they're "juicy!"

Well-made paint bars can be used in combination with traditional oils. They touch dry in two to eight days and are dry enough to varnish in about six months (longer for thick films).

Water-mixable Oils

I know, I know. Your mother told you, and your grandmother told you "Oil and water don't mix." And who wants to contravene mom and grandmom? I do.

If you add a cup of water to a cup of linseed oil in a mixing bowl, put on an apron, and give them a whirl with a whisk, grandmom is right: they won't mix very well. But if you've got the right equipment, and you know a thing or two about chemistry and making emulsions, oil and water can mix quite nicely, thank you. In fact, stable emulsions have been made from elements that don't mix through ordinary means for centuries. Millennia, even.

So, with all due respect to your grandmom and mine: get current, ma'am. Oil and water emulsions have a long history. And there's no reason they can't be used to make artists' paints and colors.

In fact, the specific techniques used today for milling the new water-mixable oils have been around for a couple of decades. It's just that nobody was interested in them. Until now. What's changed? Increased awareness of the health issues that surround solvents.

Water-mixable oils mean that artists take advantage of the qualities that come only with oil color, while completely avoiding mineral spirits and turpentine. And for many, that's a powerful advantage, particularly in school and university studio environs, where ten or twenty students may be working in a single room with open solvent containers. And if the solvent is water, it makes for a far less noxious environment (not counting what's blasting on the radio).

At present, there are at least three water-mixable oils that employ slightly different chemistry to emulsify

with water. Each manufacturer considers its own chemistry to be proprietary, so we won't even go into the specifics regarding how it's done. Let's just say that, to date, the most successful strategy—and one that produces a color that mixes and performs most like traditional oils—is one by which the oil molecule is modified slightly to accept water as a solvent. The emulsion is "self-generating" and doesn't require added chemical emulsifiers in the mix.

Note: Artisan Water Mixable Oils from Winsor & Newton are just such a color. As the market changes, and new products are developed, it's important that the artist (you) pays great attention to the literature about these paints and selects a color range that includes a minimum of added emulsifiers and that shows every indication of remaining stable and permanent.

A Few Tips for Using Water-mixable Oils

Water-mixable oils are not related, in any way or form, to watercolor. As the paint has come into more general use, it's become clear that many users believe that, because it can be thinned slightly with water, it can be used like a watercolor. No way.

Water-mixable oils are oil colors. The well-made versions mix like oils, work like oils, and smell like oils. The only difference is that, instead of requiring a strong solvent like turpentine or mineral spirits, the color will thin with a more common solvent, namely good old H$_2$O. Here are some tips for using water with water-mixable oils:

• Use as little water as possible. Just like with traditional oils, too much solvent can leave the color underbound and unstable.

• When adding water, do so slowly while stirring. This allows the emulsion to form with even consistency.

• As with traditional oils, it's better to use additive mediums to adjust the working character and consistency of your paint. Mediums give you greater control over the working properties, and you eliminate the prospect of an underbound film. It's wise to choose a water-mixable oil color that includes water-mixable mediums in the range.

The one issue with water-mixable oils that can require some "palette management" is in regard to "color shift." Water bends and refracts light differently than oil or turpentine or mineral spirits. Adding water to the color mixture can lighten the color ever-so-slightly while painting. Once the water has evapo-

A simple glass oval with a chain is perfectly suited for use as a color testing and glazing palette.

Managing the Color Shift-reversion

This dandy tip comes courtesy of Laurie Hines, Education Advisor for Winsor & Newton, in southern California. The color shift-reversion tends to be noticeable only as an appreciable volume of water is added to the water-mixable color mix. (At the risk of sounding like somebody's broken-record-mom: to ensure a stable film, be careful about adding too much!) If adding water, and to ensure that you're going to get the color and mix you're after, head for a craft store and purchase a small glass oval (about 4 inches by 6 inches), complete with a plastic or metal edge around the perimeter, and a hanging chain. This is going to be your "viewing palette."

When mixing paint to which you know you'll be adding water, brush a small bit of the mixed color (before thinning) upon your glass oval. Hold the glass at eye level, between you and the painting, and position it so you can view the mixed color as it will appear upon the surface. Then, thin the color on your palette to the desired consistency and paint away, knowing that, when dry, the color will match what you've viewed through the glass.

Extra-value bonus hint! *The same tip works magically when glazing with oils or acrylics. You can check the hue and tint of a possible glaze layer by applying the glazing color first upon the glass oval. Hold the glass at eye level and view the portion of the painting in question through the layer of color. Bingo! Instant glaze check!*

rated, the color reverts to its true character. This shift-reversion factor is minimal, but it can be disconcerting until you learn how to manage it. And it's nothing like the shift that occurs with acrylics, in which the color darkens permanently (sometimes considerably) from what came out of the tube or jar, as water evaporates from the applied film.

What About Long-term Stability?

Given that water-mixable oils are new to the market, there has been some public questioning regarding their long-term stability and the fact that they've not been evaluated by conservators. Here's what Alun Foster, Chief Chemist at Winsor & Newton, in Wealdstone, England, has to say on the matter:

"Conservators generally evaluate materials only when the paint has failed. If water-mixable oil colours don't fail, they are unlikely to ever be tested by conservators. Acrylic emulsions were not examined by conservators until very recently when problems arose due to poorly formulated products in the early sixties. There are at least three types of water-mixable oil colours on the market, so generalized statements are misleading.

"A linseed oil that has been modified to be water-mixable will behave like a normal oil. **There is no chemical reason to suspect that the modified oil is any less stable than a traditional oil.** Emulsified oils, in fact, have a history of stability going back to prehistoric times.

"The current water-mixable oils have been around for over twenty years. Developments in acrylics have pushed them into the background, but market requirements for less hazardous materials have brought them (water-mixable oils) to the fore again."

As Alun says, there's no reason to suspect that the modified oil vehicle will behave any differently than conventional oil during oxidation. And there's no reason to deprive artists who are sensitive to solvents, or that want to eliminate any and all noxious materials from their studio, from the pleasures of working with a genuine oil just because the product hasn't been—and may never be—evaluated by conservators.

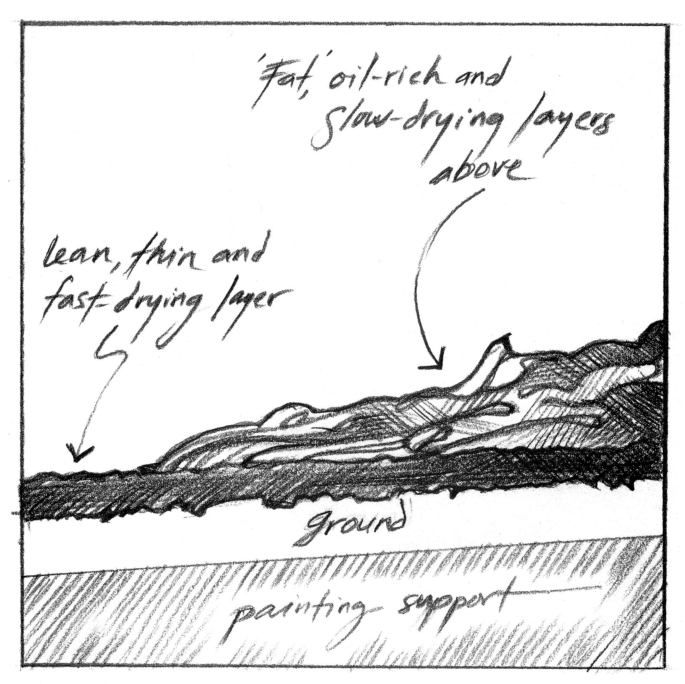

'Fat,' oil-rich and slow-drying layers above

lean, thin and fast-drying layer

ground

painting support

Each successive layer should contain progressively more oil, ensuring that the stiffer, less-flexible layers are secured between the support and the thicker, more flexible layers above.

Be Like Van Eyck!
Building the Perfect Painting

Here, item by item and step by step, is how to get the most from oils. What better place to start than…

…From the Ground Up: Fat Over Lean!

The most critical element in the stability and permanence of an oil painting is the flexibility of the film. If you've been painting with oils for longer than a week or two, you've heard of the "fat over lean" rule. I'm one of those people who always wants rules explained. I drove my parents crazy, and I'm probably about to get my comeuppance, because my children are proving to be the same kinds of demanding, explain-it-to-me individuals. So, simply articulating the "fat over lean" rule isn't going to be enough in this book. You'll be much better served if you understand why the rule applies.

By far the greatest cause of instability or cracking of oil films is from physical shock or excessive flexing; therefore, the more flexible, and the more securely bound the film, the more likely it is to "bounce back," undamaged by environmental changes (which can range from as mild as rapid shifts in temperature to as severe as a drop on the floor). The rule of "fat over lean" really means "flexible over less flexible," and it ultimately ensures that the paint layers will be as resistant as possible to shock and change. Here's how it works: layers of color that have more oil dry to a more flexible film, while those with less oil and more pigment dry to a stiffer, often more brittle state; therefore, the stiffer, more brittle layers of color should reside upon the hard ground. That's the safest place for them, because a well-constructed ground is going to hold up well against shock and will lend stability to the more fragile layer of color.

More oil should be added to each consecutive layer of color, ensuring that the layers become progressively more flexible. These increasingly flexible layers are better able to absorb shock, "rolling with the punches," so to speak. Conversely, if brittle layers are applied over oil-rich (or fat and flexible) layers of color, the result is going to be less than ideal. For, as the flexible layers move and shift below, the brittle layer above will be forced to shake and shimmy beyond its capacity and it will crack. Guaranteed.

That's the rule and reason of fat over lean, or flexible over less flexible, and it's the only way to build a painting that will be stable and secure for generations.

Choosing the Right Support

What's the most critical part of your painting? The color? The varnish? Your expressive vision? In fact, the most important part of the painting structure is in the combined stability of the support and the ground. For, if the foundation of your painting is strong and well-prepared for the ages, so too does your color and artistic image stand a good chance of surviving long-term. Conversely, the best quality color, applied in the most conscientious manner, with the most careful technique, stands little or no chance of making it until next week, let alone the next century, if the support and ground are weak, wobbly, and poised to fall apart.

It's time for a couple of definitions: The **support** is the physical structure upon which you build your painting. It may be a panel, or a canvas, or a wall, or a car. The **ground** is the primer or the gesso used to prepare the surface for application of color. For maximum stability, oils require a support that is as

strong and inflexible as possible. Here are your options:

There's no question that **panels** are the preferred choice for stability. Wood, masonite, or, if cost is not a factor, (aluminum honeycomb) panels offer proven longevity and a surface that won't flex, twist, or bend unless subjected to extraordinary circumstances. They are, however, heavier and more costly than stretched canvas.

Canvas is often a workable choice, although it will inevitably subject the paint film to more stress than color applied upon a panel. But canvas is lighter in weight, more easily transported, and offers the advantage of a stretched, responsive surface. Stretched to an appropriate tension, there's real tactile pleasure in working on a surface that gives something in return.

If canvas is your choice, and permanence is your aim, select the heaviest weight and tightest weave possible. Both variables will enhance the longevity of the support and, ultimately, of the painting. Linen canvas (also made, interestingly enough, from the artist's friend and source of linseed oil, the flax plant), makes for a tighter, more stable support than canvas made from cotton.

Make certain that the canvas is tightly stretched across heavy-duty stretchers. And, if the stretcher frame exceeds 20 inches in any direction, the frame should be cross-braced. (Note: Even in small sizes, light-duty stretchers simply don't offer adequate stability. They should be used only if you're willing to sacrifice permanence for cost.)

When opting for canvas, your choice of ground or primer becomes more important, as well.

Prime Time! Choosing a Traditional Oil Ground or Acrylic Gesso

If painting upon a panel, the question regarding acrylic gesso versus traditional size and oil ground becomes largely moot. Modern acrylic gesso, if produced as true artists' quality, is exceptionally stable and secure. And there's no reason that it can't be used with confidence as a ground upon a panel. Simply apply two or three coats (sanding lightly in between) to seal the surface and prepare it for color.

If painting on canvas, the question of acrylic versus traditional ground becomes more challenging. The traditional option of glue sizing followed by an oil-based artists' primer makes the most rigid, inflexible, and secure ground for oil on canvas. The glue

Above are single coats of two different grades of gesso. The gesso on top is low cost and much thinner, requiring multiple coats to achieve a stable ground. The gesso below is artists' quality; it's much denser and far superior to the low-cost product. Courtesy of Winsor & Newton.

A word of warning: As with everything else discussed in this book, you get what you pay for with gesso. Low-cost gessoes don't offer much in the way of covering power, and they often contain too much water, creating a ground that may be prone to cracking. Again, if permanence is your aim, select the highest quality artists' grade gesso you can afford.

A bonus word of warning: Never, ever use house paint as a primer or ground (if we were having this discussion face-to-face, this is where I'd stamp my foot and maybe even wag my finger). House paint isn't formulated for the long haul (and by that, I mean centuries-long), and it's far too absorbent. A ground that's too absorbent can, quite literally, suck the oil out of the paint film, leaving color that's underbound, unstable, and dull in color. Artists' quality gesso is formulated to offer a moderate degree of absorbency, well-suited for the more common fluid application of color when underpainting. It also offers just the right degree of texture, or "tooth," to which heavier body color can stick and stay. Low-cost primers and/or house paint aren't formulated to offer either of those two essential qualities.

size seals and stiffens the canvas support, and the primer creates a receptive surface for the color. A number of reputable manufacturers produce both glue size and **artists' oil primer**. Simply follow the usage instructions provided upon the label.

Rabbit skin glue has been used for centuries as a canvas size, with **PVA (polyvinyl acetate)** coming into more recent vogue. Because it's more stable, and because hide or skin glues undergo expansion and contraction depending upon humidity and atmospheric conditions, PVA is the better choice. Golden Artist Colors also produces an acrylic medium that is far stiffer than most (GAC 400) and that can be used as an effective size.

Today's artists' oil primers are formulated for more rapid drying than the lead white/linseed oil primer used for centuries, and that required months to dry before painting.

Acrylic gesso has the advantage of being simpler to apply, and it also provides a perfectly receptive surface for the color. Its disadvantage, however, is in its flexibility. Acrylics are, by nature, more flexible than oils. So, when applying oil color over acrylic gesso upon canvas, you've already violated the rule of flexible over less flexible. The problem can be mitigated by applying a number of layers of gesso—as many as four or five—and building a thick, rigid surface. To ensure good adhesion, it's wise to sand each layer lightly before applying the next. (Not forgetting, of course, to wear a mask!)

This is a good time to reiterate a point made earlier about when and how you opt for permanence. It's your choice. As a writer and art-material guy, it's not my place to declare that all art should be made using the highest quality, most permanent products available. It is my place, however, to ensure that you, dear reader, have the information necessary to make informed choices. There will be instances in which you choose lower cost, or ease of application over maximum permanence. But, after reading this book (if I've done my job), you'll know exactly what you're doing, as well as the long-term implications when you choose your tools and materials.

Building the Color Layers

Now that you're facing a clean, pristine, achingly-ready-for-paint surface—whether it's on a panel or a canvas, or primed through traditional methods or with acrylic gesso—you've got a choice to make. Do you want to work slowly and build

layers, or are you going to create the painting "alla prima," all at once, in a single layer? Or a combination of both?

Either approach is viable, as long as you keep in mind a few rules of thumb:

• **When underpainting, choose transparent, faster drying colors thinned with no more than 30 percent solvent.** (More on drying times later.) If you wish to accelerate the drying of this layer, add an alkyd-based painting medium to the mix. (For a complete discussion on solvents, see page 55.)

• **A word about underpainting with acrylics.** Even though acrylics are commonly used for an underpainting layer beneath oils, it's not a good practice. As acrylic colors dry, they typically create a layer that is much smoother and lacking in the tooth or absorption than is needed for stable adhesion of a subsequent oil layer. And, because acrylics are more flexible than oils, underpainting with acrylics is an automatic violation of the "flexible over less flexible" rule. If you're working in oils, it's best to stick to oils for all layers of the painting. If you desire a faster drying color for use with underpainting, then alkyd fast-drying oils are a terrific option. And they are highly receptive to subsequent layers of traditional oils.

• **Use mediums to adjust and manage the viscosity and character of the paint.** Color can be used directly from the tube for stiff, impasto applications. But consider straight color a "lean" layer, and it shouldn't be applied over other medium-rich or oil-rich "fat" layers. If you want to build impasto layers over other layers, you're better served adding an impasto medium to your color.

There is a wide variety of mediums that allows you to build layers of color, in different viscosities. Use them. (There's more coming up on mediums.) Adding mediums to color makes the layer fatter and more oil-rich.

• **In the middle layers, add solvent directly to your painting medium, but not directly into the color.** The solvent volume within your additive medium shouldn't exceed 20 to 30 percent.

• **In the top-most layer of colors, avoid solvent all together.** Adjust your working characteristics with mediums only.

• **Use only enough medium to do the job.** Remember our exercise in Chapter 4, in which we added too much Stand oil to a fast-drying color and waited for it to wrinkle? A little bit goes a long way.

• **Use one medium at a time.** Adding one medium to speed drying and another to increase flow is likely to cause problems. Too many mediums means too many drying processes, and different rates of expansion and contraction, within the body of the color. There is a wide variety of mediums that does different combinations of things: speed drying with increased flow, slow drying with increased flow, and stiffer body with faster drying. Choose a medium that combines the qualities you're after.

• **Avoid driers.** There are agents, like cobalt drier, that can be added to the color to speed drying, but they tend to embrittle the paint film. Now that we've got fast-drying alkyd-based mediums easily available, there's not much need for adding driers directly to your color.

• **Consider some colors fatter than others.** Early on, we talked about how pigments absorb oil in different ways during milling. Some absorb more, others less. This has lots of implications, but most immediate is the fact that some colors come out of the tube in dispersion with more oil. And more oil means fatter color. How do you tell? Colors that come out of the tube with a high gloss sheen have more oil than colors that appear more matte. And, when needed, you can adjust lean colors to a fatter state by adding medium.

• **Avoid thick underlayers of color.** In general, stick with a principle of thick over thin when building color layers. Thick layers below, because of varying expansion and contraction rates during drying, can cause thinner layers above to crack. Your thickest layers should be on top.

• **Pay attention to the drying rates of your colors, applying slower-drying colors over fast-drying colors.** For a variety of reasons, different

Colors used in underpainting should be thinned with no more than 30 percent solvent. Adding an alkyd-based medium to the mix will help accelerate the drying of your underpainting layer.

colors dry at different rates. Some reach a touch-dry state in a day or two, while others may take two weeks. And, again, because of varying rates of expansion and contraction, slow-drying underlayers can cause fast-drying layers above to crack. **In general, problems can be minimized by avoiding any broadly applied, thick, continuous, slow-drying layers of color in your underpaintings. And allow each layer to touch-dry before building another.** Reputable manufacturers will provide you with a list within their literature of drying rates for their colors.

Mediums at Large: What Do They Do?

Here, in a simple list, are the most common mediums and what you can expect from each:

Alkyd mediums. Because of their versatility and speed of drying, these have become the most popular mediums since their introduction a few years ago. There are alkyd mediums offered by a wide variety of manufacturers. Here are a few of the most readily available:
• **Liquin** (Winsor & Newton), the first alkyd medium, speeds drying, improves flow. It's ideal for glazing.
• **Wingel** (Winsor & Newton) is an alkyd medium that speeds drying and improves flow with a slightly stiffer consistency.
• **Oleopasto** (Winsor & Newton) speeds drying and stiffens the color considerably for impasto applications.
• **Galkyd mediums** (Gamblin Artists Colors) offer a variety of similar characteristics.

Drying oils. These are the oils used as the vehicle in milling. Just like prepared mediums, drying oils can be used to change the consistency, the working characteristics, and the drying time of colors.
• **Cold-pressed linseed oil** reduces the consistency, improves flow, and increases gloss and transparency.
• **Refined linseed oil** slows drying while offering qualities comparable to those from cold-pressed linseed oil.
• **Stand oil** is ideal for glazing. It levels the color, is resistant to yellowing, and improves the durability of the color film. It's also slow-drying.
• **Bleached linseed oil** is pale in color and well-suited for use with light tints. It speeds drying and improves flow.
• **Thickened linseed oil** speeds drying more than the Bleached variety. It improves flow, gloss, and the durability of the film.

• **Drying linseed oil** promotes faster drying than any of its brethren and increases gloss.
• **Drying poppy oil** speeds drying and is suited for light tints.

The Varnished Truth: Where, When, and How to Varnish

For the long-term protection of your work and your vision, varnishing is essential. And it's equally important that it be done correctly. With all of the skill and effort that you've invested, the last thing you want to do is undermine your permanent paint film by varnishing too soon, or with an inappropriate varnish.

Varnishing too soon can lead to all kinds of problems. The varnish can sink into the still-wet surface, making the paint film sensitive to solvent, or the varnish may turn tacky and sticky. In short, it's important to varnish only when the paint film is ready. So, how do you know when you can varnish?

Testing for Readiness

Conventional oils require six months to fully dry—often longer for thick films. Same for water-mixable oils. Alkyds require a good month of dry-time before varnishing. You can test for readiness by gently rubbing a corner of your painting with a soft, solvent-soaked rag. If no color appears upon the rag, then the film is truly dry and the painting is ready for varnishing. If color appears, then wait a bit longer. You can, if needed, apply a retouching or temporary varnish until the painting is ready for the final varnish (see the next column).

If the painting continues, long after the six-month mark, to show color that isn't fully dry, then you may need to consider whether or not the film has "sunk." Sinking means that the oil film, for whatever reason, is unable to fully dry, either because the oil has been pulled from the paint layer by a too-absorbent ground, or the paint film was overthinned to begin with and is now underbound. Sinking can be rectified through a procedure called "oiling out" (see the next column), and the painting can then varnished.

The Varnish Ideal

A varnish should do the following:
• Dry to a hard, non-sticky film that protects your painting surface.
• Offer great clarity and remain non-yellowing over time.

• Be easily removable (while leaving the paint film beneath untouched) should new varnish be needed, or if the painting requires some measure of repair or TLC sometime in the distant future.

Until recently, varnishing involved trade-offs. A varnish that offered great clarity initially might go yellow later on, or prove difficult to remove. Within the last few years, however, varnishes have been developed that meet all of the above criteria quite well. Conserv-Art varnishes from Winsor & Newton and Gamvar varnish from Gamblin Artists Colors are examples of new technology and new chemistry that yield better varnishes than ever before.

Temporary, Isolating, or Retouching Varnishes

If you need to varnish a painting before it's fully dry, use an isolating or retouching varnish. The painting must be allowed to dry for at least a month before the temporary varnish is applied, and then must be allowed to fully dry before a final varnish. An isolating or retouching varnish does not require removal before applying the final varnish.

Oiling Out

As mentioned previously, there are instances in which it becomes clear that the paint film is underbound, either because the ground is too absorbent, or the paint was overthinned to begin with. The telltale sign of sunken color is an area of paint that loses its sheen and goes quite matte. To be sure, test the area using the technique outlined above when checking for varnish readiness.

Oiling out is simply a technique to restore enough oil to the film so it can fully bind and dry. Mix a small percentage of solvent (no more than 10 to 20 percent by volume) with stand oil. With a soft cloth, gently rub the oil mixture into the sunken area of color. Wipe off any excess oil and allow the painting to set for a day or two. If the area goes flat and matte again, repeat the process until it regains a sheen comparable to surrounding, healthier areas. Allow to fully dry and then varnish.

What's "Alla Prima?"

This is an Italian term for working the painting surface quickly, often finishing it in one session. Working *alla prima* requires great immediacy and can be great fun. Obviously, because you've no time to allow layers to dry, you'll be working with a single layer of color. And, as long as you keep the guide-

lines provided earlier for building a stable film, the painting can be perfectly stable. When working wet color into wet color (called wet-into-wet, cleverly enough), remember to use but a single medium in your color mix.

Painting on Non-traditional Surfaces

Oils can be used on virtually anything, as long as the surface is dry, stable, inflexible, and can be adequately primed. Remember that the durability of the painting will be only as long as the surface or structure itself. If smooth, the surface should be cleaned and sanded so as to provide adequate adhesion and then primed with an oil painting primer or gesso. The finished painting should be allowed to dry and then varnished appropriately.

Choosing the Right Brush for Oil Color

There's really only one benchmark for brushes used with thick or viscous color: The thicker the color, the stiffer the brush tuft.

Think about it. A heavy paint, like oils or acrylics straight from the tube, requires a brush with enough resilience to mash and bash the color about. A color that has been thinned slightly requires a softer tuft. And a color that has been thinned to a fluid consistency requires a brush with some flow control.

Here are the common hairs and filaments used with brushes for thick color:

The Well-Dressed Hog

How are pigs and Kolinskies the same? In addition to a striking similarity in the number of legs, they both produce hair that makes the very best brush tuft of its kind. Fine hog bristle is as good for use with thick paint as Kolinsky is with watercolor.

What's the difference between pigs and Kolinskies? Hog hair comes much cheaper. The finest bristle brush in a large size may be somewhere around $20. Conversely, the finest, large Kolinsky brush requires a sprightly leap into three figures.

The very best bristle comes from Chinese hogs—Chungking, to be exact—where the bristles are most resilient and dressed to perfection. They're processed in lengths as long as 8 inches. After being boiled and bleached, only the white bristles are used for professional-quality brushes.

In addition to the resiliency, the most important characteristic of fine bristle is the "flagged," or split,

Replica of a brush from the early nineteenth century. Courtesy of Winsor & Newton.

end. Flags carry more color on the brush tuft and then apply it evenly to the surface. The very best brushes have upwards of 80 percent flagged bristles and, rather than being neat and crisply trimmed, they sport a frizzy, Einstein-ish look.

Badger to the Bone!

Softer-than-hog badger hair is perfect for use with moderately thinned colors. And it has no peer when used for blending oils or acrylics. The hair is conical with a belly close to the tip. Consequently, the brush tuft is as bushy as an Airedale's eyebrow.

Mongoose hair is comparable, although increasingly difficult to obtain. A number of manufacturers now offer excellent synthetic filament brushes that closely replicate the performance of natural badger or mongoose hair.

Same Ol' Sable

Red sable or weasel is often used as a brush tuft for oils and acrylics that have been thinned to a watercolor-like consistency. You'll never find a top-grade Kolinsky hair in an oil painting brush, however. It's simply not worth subjecting valuable Kolinsky to the abuse that comes with solvents and rough surfaces.

Handles: The Long and Short

Why the long handles on brushes for acrylics or oils? A long-handled "easel brush" allows you to stand far away from the canvas surface and survey how the entire piece is evolving as you work.

Acrylic Color

Acrylic is everywhere. It's in our clothes, our cars, our eyeglasses, and even in the airplane seat within which I'm right this very moment comfortably (kind of) ensconced. And, when compared to oil or watercolors, acrylic paints are a different animal altogether.

Since their introduction more than fifty years ago, acrylics have been labeled as a really fast-drying alternative to oil colors. Or as a really waterproof alternative to watercolors. And, while acrylics can quite effectively wear a multitude of "hats," it's unfair to view them solely in comparison to other media. It's because of their astonishing versatility, and because they can approximate the characteristics of other media, that their full potential is still being explored. I can't quite shake this feeling that, in fifty years, we'll be talking about painting in a completely new context. And it will be, in part, because of the versatility and the not-yet-envisioned applications that will evolve with acrylic emulsion colors. That, and a little thing called the graphics computer. (More on that in the next chapter.)

So, what is really, truly unique about acrylics?

Doing It All: The Most Versatile Medium

With all due respect to those who use acrylics as oil or watercolor wannabes, the true strengths of the medium lie elsewhere. Over the last few years, oil colors have become safer—with less toxic solvents as well as the new and very workable water soluble oils. And alkyd-based oil colors offer a much faster drying option for oil painters, as well. These advances truly obviate the need to see acrylics as some sort of fast-drying oil color alternative.

The true strengths of acrylics, at least as we currently understand them, lie in their ability to go from high fluidity to thick viscosity, all the while retaining the true character of the pigment carried within. To get watercolor, oil, or tempera to a state of high fluidity, you invariably are forced to spread the pigment load, increasing the transparency of the film. Not so with acrylics. A highly fluid color, applied in large volumes, is possible that retains the optimal pigment load and relative opacity.

At the other end of the viscosity spectrum, acrylics can be made to act as the most sculptural of all media. With the use of high-viscosity color, or through the addition of the right additive mediums,

"PRESS 1999," by Susanna Starr, sponge/acrylic paint, 51 x 60 x 144 inches. Susanna Starr's work is one example of the unique expressive qualities that are possible only with acrylic colors. PRESS 1999 clearly illustrates that acrylics can be sculptural as well as two-dimensional. Starr works with large industrial sponges, saturating them with gallons upon gallons of acrylic color, and then allowing the combined forces of gravity and hydrodynamics to make a joyful and quite random counterpoint to the monolithic sponge figures.

the paint takes on a heavy, thick-bodied consistency that remains easily manipulated. All that, and the color can be applied to virtually any surface.

And all of this happens, not because of the volume of solvent within the mix, but because of the nature of the acrylic resin and how it functions within an emulsion with water.

Interestingly enough, at the time that I write these words, I happen to be aboard an airplane, in a window seat on an astonishingly clear day, directly above the Grand Canyon. It seems only fitting that I write about the sculptural nature of acrylic colors while looking down upon one of the most colorful and sculptural vistas on our planet.

What Is It? And Where Did It Come From?

Acrylics were first developed in the 1940s by a couple of true pioneers, Leonard Bocour and his nephew, Sam Golden. Their first product created with the newly available acrylic resins was called "Magna color," and it came directly as the result of an ongoing dialog in Bocour's New York colorshop with artists like Morris Louis and Barnett Newman, who were looking for colors that would give them greater dynamic fluidity.

As Golden and Bocour continued to explore the potential of the new vehicle, they were eventually able to formulate an entire range of color for artists, with dependable working and pigment characteristics. Acrylics have since become the most popular color medium for artists and craftspeople the world over. It's interesting to note that the meteoric growth of the art community in the 1950s and '60s, and of the craft industry a decade or two later, both correspond to the development of an easily applied, water-soluble, and easy-clean-up paint. While there's no question that there are other factors that have contributed to that growth, it's hard to imagine the almost universal degree of art in public education, not to mention painted sweatshirts and decorated milk bottles, without acrylic colors.

Acrylics are made up of three basic constituents: acrylic polymer resin, water (in an emulsion with the polymer), and pigment. (Remember what a polymer is? It's a chain made up of identical (or virtually identical) "monomers" or constituent pieces.)

In short, the acrylic resin is put into a stable emulsion with water and then milled with pigment. When the paint is applied to the surface and exposed to atmosphere, the water evaporates or is absorbed into the painting ground below. As water leaves the emulsion, each acrylic monomer can position itself for bonding with a neighboring monomer. And as each monomer bonds to its neighbor, forming a strong, stable, and highly structural film, they conveniently lock each and every particle of pigment into place.

There is an almost infinite number of things that can be done to change how the monomers move and fit with each other during the state before they dry. And that's the key to the color's versatility. The chemistry can be managed so that the acrylic monomers become very slippery and fluid, making for a highly fluid, and still highly concentrated, color. Or the chemistry of the paint can be adjusted to make a paint body that's quite stiff and sculptural. Or high gloss. Or low gloss. Or anything in between.

The Next Generation

The key to making great acrylics is, in addition to the quality of the pigment, in the use of the ideal acrylic resin. And there are lots to choose from. Manufacturers such as Liquitex, Golden, and Winsor & Newton have invested untold sums of money and resources into looking for acrylic resins that offer the greatest clarity, adhesion, and stability.

Early acrylics weren't without their problems. There were justifiable concerns with stability and color change. But, thanks to some very dedicated and skilled chemists in labs across the world, those issues have been all but eliminated. Modern acrylics offer great stability and clarity, and can be used with confidence that they're going to be around for the long haul.

Building the Perfect Acrylic Painting

Here's a rundown on how to build a stable acrylic painting, from the support and ground up...

Choosing the Right Support

While some of the same issues apply when discussing supports and grounds for oils and acrylics, there are some salient differences, as well. Because acrylics are, by nature, more flexible than oils, they can be applied to a wider array of surfaces. Depending upon your chosen surface, just remember that, prior to applying color or a ground, the surface must be clean, dry, and stable itself.

If working upon a smooth, non-porous surface,

Acrylic color is capable of dramatic, high-peak, sculptural surfaces. Here, phthalocyanine blue has been adjusted to a stiffer consistency with different mediums. On the left, the color has been altered with modeling paste, and on the right with impasto medium. Both yield a high-peak surface, but the color takes on a chalky appearance with the modeling paste, while remaining more true with the impasto medium. Courtesy of Winsor & Newton.

abrading is necessary to ensure good adhesion. On most metal or wood surfaces, sanding or scuffing can be perfectly adequate, while glass may well require sand-blasting.

If working upon a wall or some other mural application, make certain that the surface is free of mildew by washing thoroughly with a solution of household bleach (one part) and water (three parts).

Metal surfaces should be degreased with isopropyl (rubbing) alcohol. And always treat any solvent or cleaning solution with care, wearing safety glasses when appropriate.

Priming the Surface

To prime or not to prime. Even though the stiffness of the ground is not as critical when using acrylics rather than oils, priming is still a good idea. To ensure a surface that offers the ideal combination of absorbency and tooth, a layer of acrylic gesso is desirable. If you're looking for the bleeding and staining qualities that come with working upon raw canvas or fabric, then the final image should be varnished or covered with a layer of clear acrylic medium.

Gessoes and Grounds

Over the last decade, an astonishing variety of gessoes has hit the market. In addition to conventional gesso, there are hard sandable gessoes, clear gessoes, colored gessoes, absorbent grounds, and more. And, because of the high level of technical expertise within the industry, these gessoes and grounds, as long as they're used in accordance with the manufacturers' instructions, can be used with confidence in regard to their stability. So experiment and enjoy.

As mentioned earlier, high-quality artists' grade gesso should always be used. Low-cost gessoes often

contain too little acrylic and too much water. And, where a layer or two of high-quality gesso may be perfectly sufficient, repeated layers of a low-cost gesso may be required to achieve a reasonably opaque surface. In the end, because of the volume and layers required, a low-cost gesso may cost just as much as a higher-quality product. And all of those layers mean more work. It's pretty clear: low-cost gesso is no bargain.

A word about water. Remember that the stability of the acrylic film depends upon all of those little acrylic monomers being able to link up into a polymer structure. And, as discussed in a previous chapter, too much water in the mix can hinder those linkages. So, if using more than just a splash of water to thin your color, always add acrylic medium to the mix, as well. Doing so ensures that the volume of acrylic remains high enough to ensure stable film formation.

Color Shift

Because of the volume of water within the acrylic emulsion, color shift is an issue. Water bends and refracts light differently than the acrylic resin, often creating a slight shift in color value as the water evaporates and the acrylic vehicle goes from milky white to clear. The color generally goes slightly darker, and there's no question that managing the color shift can be a challenge when working in acrylics.

Mediums

Gels and pastes and pumice mediums, oh my! Companies like Liquitex and Golden, that specialize in acrylics only, bring more additive mediums, that do more things, to market every year. If you want to slow the drying, speed the drying, add sand or grit or glass to the texture, maybe even walk the dog and take out the trash, you can do it with acrylic additive

This color includes a pumice medium for added texture.

mediums. And, perhaps more than anything else, all of these options staring at the artist from the retail shelf may ensure that acrylics are finally seen for what they are: a paint with its own characteristics, its own advantages, and a very different range of capabilities than any other product on the market.

Rather than itemizing all of the different kinds of mediums on the market—a list that will, I'm sure, continue to grow over the coming years—it makes sense to identify a category or three into which the mediums can be identified:

Viscosity mediums. The majority of mediums fall into this camp, a group of additives that adjusts the viscosity of color right out of the tube or pot. These mediums are available in matte or gloss surfaces, and they can take the paint from low, fluid viscosity, to high-peak, heavy viscosity. There are fluid mediums, gel mediums, heavy gel mediums, and light and heavy modeling pastes. And everything else in between.

Added texture mediums. These are gel mediums that contain a variety of additives, such as sand, pumice, fiber, glass beads, and more.

Drying and other additives. Acrylics dry fast. Really fast. And while you'll never get the color to dry slowly enough to allow for continued reworking over a long period of time (like you can with oils), there are **retarder** additives to slow things down a bit. Additives like retarders adjust the chemical and working properties of the paint, but they don't include acrylic emulsion themselves. Because they don't offer their own binding properties, they should be used sparingly, in volumes only enough to gain the desired effect. In addition to retarders, for slowing drying and increasing open time, there are **flow enhancers** to loosen up the paint and allow it to spread rapidly (like Ox Gall with watercolor), some thickeners, and products to enable other techniques, like **marbling** or **monoprinting**.

Interference Colors

Acrylics can often support pigments that won't go readily into suspension in other vehicles. Like that strange and fun breed of paint: interference colors. Look from one direction and it has a sheen of one color; change your angle and it takes on another hue. The possibilities are intoxicating. These colors can be used for conventional painting; they're fabulous for jewelry making and other less traditional applications.

How do they work? The pigment is composed of mica that has been coated with titanium dioxide. Light waves reflect off of the mica and the titanium layer at one color frequency while another color just passes right through. The thickness of the titanium layer dictates the colors. With a thick titanium layer, for example, you see reflective green at one angle and red at the other. That's interference green. A thinner layer means different reflections and interference gold.

The Varnished Truth

There's a common misconception that finished acrylic paintings do not require varnishing. Wrong. For a variety of reasons, acrylic paintings will benefit from a coat of varnish, most importantly the dirt and dust factor. When dry, most acrylics retain a tacky surface, particularly under conditions of high heat and humidity. And that stickiness, no matter how slight, is guaranteed to pick up dirt and dust from the atmosphere, leaving an even coat of grime covering your painting, a coat that's not easy to remove. So, varnishing is critical.

The same rules apply for varnishing acrylic paintings that apply with oils. The varnish should dry clear, be resistant to yellowing, and it should be removable.

The Ongoing Evolution of Acrylic Color

There continues to be noticeable improvements in the working properties and stability of acrylic colors. For example, a few years ago, Winsor & Newton introduced Finity Artists' Acrylic colors and promoted the fact that the range featured a lessened color shift from wet to dry, and was noticeably less tacky when dry. And it's nice to see these claims borne out and proven to be more than just marketing tag lines.

Recently, when the Tate Gallery in London was looking for an acrylic color for restoration of a sculpture produced in the 1960s by Philip King, Finity Artists' Acrylics were selected because of superior pigment strength and the least degree of dirt pickup and retention. Other well-known brands were tested and dismissed because the dry, yet still-tacky, surface accumulated an unacceptable amount dust and dirt. Bottom line? There are times when you can believe those marketing-types when they tell you a product is better.

This letter opener was painted with interference and metallic acrylic colors.

Some manufacturers produce specialized varnishes just for acrylic paintings. Others recommend the use of an acrylic soft gel medium as a final varnish. Golden Artist Colors goes as far as recommending an isolating coat of varnish (a mixture of soft gel medium [gloss] with water) prior to the final coat.

Regardless of your chosen varnish, it's wise to read the manufacturer's instructions for varnishing and follow them carefully. And, when varnishing over an absorbent surface (such as raw canvas or wood, or over an absorbent gesso or ground), it's wise to use a gloss varnish rather than matte. Varnishes with matting agents can separate, with the varnish and solvent being absorbed into the painting surface, leaving the matting agent upon the surface. If you do choose to use a matte varnish over an absorbent ground, then a middle, isolating varnish as noted above is essential.

Mixing and Matching

Check out my painting table, and I bet it's just like yours. There are tubes from a variety of different manufacturers strewn from one end to the next. And, while that's perfectly appropriate when working in oils or watercolors, it's not always the best idea when working in acrylics. Because different manufacturers select different emulsions, that often dry differently, it's wise to do one of two things:
• Select and stick with products from a single manufacturer, or
• Do a quick test of different manufacturers' products when combined with one another. If you're adding a new color or product from a different manufacturer to your palette, apply a test mixture to a sample board. If the mixture blisters or peels, the vehicles aren't compatible.

A Word About Brushes

Your choice of brushes for use with acrylics depends entirely upon how you'll be using the color. If using the color in a thick, viscous state, right out of the tube, then choose your brush based upon the criteria outlined in the brush section for oils (see page 115). If using the color in a highly fluid state, then choose your brush based upon the criteria outlined in the brush section for watercolors (see page 99).

It's wise to use synthetic brushes with acrylics. Natural hair brushes, because of the scales that ring the hair, over load with acrylic and are difficult to wash fully clean. Synthetic brushes tend to load more evenly with acrylics, wash clean more easily, and last longer than natural hair brushes.

A word of warning: Because of how rapidly acrylics dry, always keep your brushes rinsed clean of color. Once the acrylic sets in the brush, it's very difficult, if not impossible, to get it out.

Sympathetic to Synthetic

As you might imagine, synthetic filaments behave differently with acrylics or oil colors. Because surface tension is different in an acrylic solution, the paint flows differently from the brush than does watercolor. Those nylon brushes that dispense fluid watercolor so clumsily are, in fact, perfect for moderately thinned acrylic. Taklon synthetic is produced in a wide range of diameters with varying "springiness" and can accommodate oils or acrylics from thick to thin.

In short, a bristle or stiff synthetic brush is perfect when using heavy color right out of the tube. As you let the color down, or thin it moderately, a medium-soft synthetic or natural hair (like badger) should be just right. As you thin the color to more fluid consistency, make the move to a soft synthetic or natural hair brush.

Other Media: Encaustic, Tempera, and Fresco

A book is supposed to be exhaustive and complete, right? It should offer everything there is to know about a particular subject. While that would be nice, and, as much as I would have liked to put together a book that offered every bit of information known about color and paints, it's simply not possible. So, I've had to pick and choose. And my criteria has been to select a body of information that is of universal value (how paints are made and pigment and vehicle characteristics), as well as information about the application of the most popular mediums.

As much as I would like to go into detail about painting with encaustic (pigment mixed with heated wax) or egg tempera or traditional plaster wall fresco, there simply isn't room in this volume. My sincere hope is that this book will help artists working in all mediums. But for specific information about application and techniques in encaustic, tempera, and fresco, I must recommend other sources: *The Artist's Handbook*, by Ralph Mayer (Viking, New York, revised edition, 1991), offers excellent application and technical information regarding encaustic, tempera, and fresco. *The Painter's Handbook*, by

Mark Gottsegen (Watson Guptill, NY, 1993), is an excellent source of detailed reference information. In the UK, a fine resource is *Artists' Materials: Which, Why and How*, by Emma Pearce (A&C Black, London, 1992).

The March of Technology: Heat-set Artists' Colors

If we've learned any lessons at all over the twenty-five thousand years since a particularly bright Cro-Magnon guy made the first discovery that a mixture of animal fat and colored dirt will stick permanently to a rock wall, I would hope that we've learned not to ignore new ideas.

In 1997, a new kind of artists' color was brought to market. A range of pigments had been milled upon a traditional triple-roll mill, but with a vehicle quite different than any before seen in the art materials community: a polymer that hardens when subjected to heat. Once again, as Robert Gamblin has noted, virtually all of the raw materials in this community come from other industries, and our creative engineering comes in how we adapt those materials to the unique needs of our customers. Genesis Artist Colors are no exception.

According the Steve Golden, Market Developer for Genesis (now owned and marketed by Amaco), the heat-set vehicle has been used for years in medicine as a material for bone replacement. While Genesis is still in the process of documenting the long-term permanence and stability of the vehicle, the durability required for artificial bone replacement seems like a reasonable place to start.

The workability of the color is similar to that of oils, but with unlimited open time. The artist has the option of working and reworking the painting surface indefinitely, drying the surface with a heat gun only when ready. The artist also has the option of working very quickly, repeatedly glazing one layer over another much more rapidly than when working in oils or even acrylics.

According to Golden, the pigments are all category I in lightfastness (although it would be nice to see Genesis publish a composition list of the pigments, identifying each in terms of ASTM lightfast category and chemical names). Clean-up is easy, or doesn't have to be done at all because the colors don't dry in the brushes or upon the palette.

Will Genesis find a permanent home in artists' studios? There's only one individual that can answer that, and it's not me. It's the customer. Just like it was the customer that finally determined the viability of acrylic colors, oil, and watercolors, and even the colors that found their way onto cave walls twenty-five thousand years ago. Nevertheless, the ingenuity and dedication required to bring a completely new medium to market is significant and welcome.

Mixing It Up: When and How to Mix Media

The best rule of thumb when using more than one media in a single piece is to **always avoid applying a new media over the top of a media that has not completely dried and cured**. An example is the application of acrylic borne colors with oil borne media. Because oil colors must always have some atmospheric exposure and never completely dry, acrylic or water borne media should never be applied over oils. It's a bad, bad, bad thing to do. The resulting paint film will eventually degrade, delaminate, and become highly unstable. Because of variances in the flexibility of the films, the opposite is also true: oils shouldn't be applied over acrylics.

Conversely, if one medium has completely cured, and will offer adequate adhesion for a new medium, then go ahead. For example, pastels can be easily applied over watercolor on paper, or over a sanded, or toothed, acrylic film.

Different fluid media, such as oils and acrylics, should never be directly mixed. The mixture of two different carrier mediums (that polymerize or interlock upon drying through distinctly different chemical mechanisms) can inhibit either medium from forming a permanent paint film. And watercolor shouldn't be added directly to acrylics. On the other hand, because both employ the same vehicle, watercolor can be mixed with gouache. And oils within the same family—such as traditional oils, alkyds, and paint bars—may be safely intermixed.

The Bottom Line

Before moving on to the final chapters, now is a good time to sum up a couple of essential principles. All of these words, anecdotes, and illustrations have been selected to make two key points:

First, the character of the tools you choose will show up in your images. Oil is uniquely suited for some expressive choices, while acrylics are better for others, and watercolor is better for yet others. Encaustic gives you options not possible with oils, and egg tempera offers yet other choices. This also means that it's to your distinct advantage to buy the best quality products you can afford.

Second, the better you understand those tools, the more successfully (and enjoyably) you'll be able to exploit their unique qualities. And the better you'll make art.

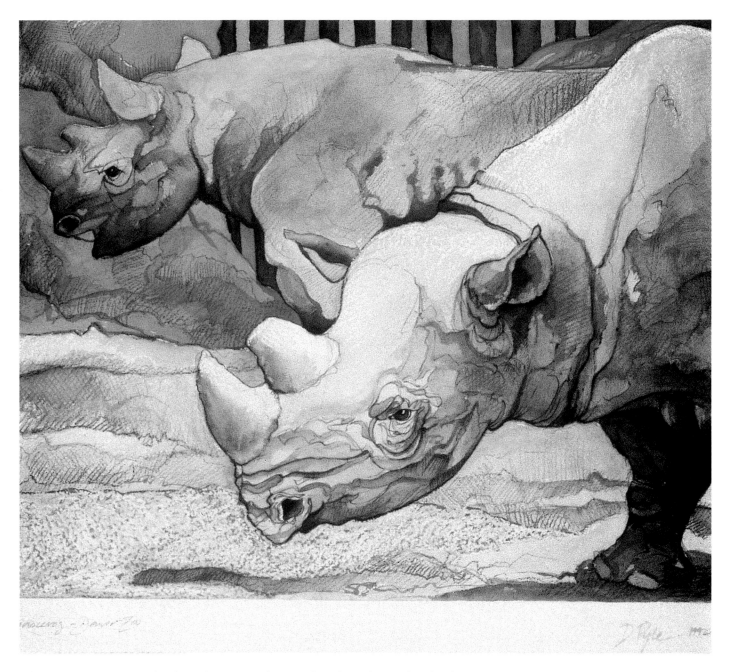

"Rhinoceros, Denver Zoo," by the author, watercolor, pastel, and graphite on handmade paper. Mixing media allows the artist to create surface texture and depth not always possible with a single medium.

Chapter 6
The Virtual Paintbrush: Art and Computers

When is a pencil like a computer? Before answering that, I need to come clean. Here are my...

...Confessions As an Early Adopter

I'm compulsive about new technology. A couple of years ago, I bought one of those ill-fated Apple Newtons, the one-pound, hand-held computer that recognizes handwriting, keeps my calendar, and feeds my dogs from anyplace on the planet. Along with stacks of papers, canvas, brushes, and tubes of color, there are banks of computers, scanners, CD-ROM drives, video machines, and digitizing tablets shoe-horned into my studio office. At dinner parties, when the conversation turns to our wired and electronic future, my wife will inevitably lean toward a companion and whisper, "You have to be careful about anything David says; he's (this is where her eyes roll) an early adopter."

So what's an early adopter? It's a term that's come into common usage in the technology arena to describe an individual who will buy a product soon after release, often before the real value of the product has been proven, certainly long before a product is accepted into wide use by the general public. We early adopters are easily seduced by anything that scores high on the "cool" scale. We love gizmos, gadgets, and thingamabobs, and some folks think P.T. Barnum had a few choice words to say about early adopters being born every minute. Others see early adopters as the canaries in the mine, providing the first indicators about the survival of a new process or tool.

At a recent meeting, I spent a good portion of my time showing off digitized pictures of my kids on my Newton device. I even convinced a few fortunate people to watch video clips of the children on my laptop computer. And, after showing the digital snap-

shots and video to one lucky woman, she turned to an innocent bystander and said, "Hey lookit this! David Pyle is scrapbooking on his computer!"

I stopped dead. She was right! I wasn't just boring people with pictures of my children—I was pointing the way to a new trend. I couldn't wait to tell my wife. "I'm not an early adopter, sweetheart; I'm a cyber-memory booker!"

In the art community—where we use tools that come with a history measured in centuries rather than weeks—it's easy to dismiss new tools or technology. But what would have happened had van Eyck not been willing to explore the qualities of the then brand-new mixture called oil color? Or the painters willing to try watercolors in the first tubes from Winsor & Newton? Or the handful of artists willing to tackle working with a new color called acrylics from Lenny Bocour, Sam Golden, Henry Levinson, and the other color pioneers of the 1940s?

Earlier, in Chapter 1, I mentioned my head-in-the-sand misperception regarding how the Macintosh would affect the commercial and graphic arts industry. I've since learned the error of my ways. And, after spending a good deal of time learning the ins and outs of Adobe Photoshop, Adobe Premiere, and Fractal Design's Painter—not to mention taking countless walks down the halls of art colleges and watching the students staring intently at computer monitors—I've no doubt that there are equally broad implications for the fine art end of the creative spectrum.

In fact, the computer IS a pencil. Or a paintbrush. It's a tool, just like any other tool used for making images. And, just like the Cro-Magnon guys discovered twenty-five millennia ago, every tool brings something unique to the image-making process.

"MANSION INTERIOR" by Jason McQuitty, working in Adobe Illustrator 8.0.

Adobe Systems is once again a proud sponsor of the Denver International Film Festival

©1999 Art Works Studio

"Cinematic Prelude" by Joe Jones. A computer is a visual tool with specific strengths and weaknesses, just like any other tool artists have been using for the last twenty-five thousand years. Asked how he created "Cinematic Prelude," Jones says, "From thumbnails, I started in Adobe Illustrator 8.0, then worked in MetaCreations—Ray Dream Studio 5, Poser 3, Bryce 4, and then completed it in Adobe Photoshop 5.0. Lots-o-work! Of course, this piece was originally inspired by the wonderful work of Maxfield Parrish." (Jones teaches digital art at the Rocky Mountain College of Art and Design, and the additional images in this chapter are from his students.)

The Computer As a Fine Art Tool

My greatest concern as I write this chapter is that it will be out of date as soon as it's published. Maybe even before. That said, here are a few things that all artists should understand about making art on a computer, along with a look into the crystal ball.

Color on the Computer

This isn't going to be a discussion on the ins and outs of individual software applications. Rather, this brief chapter will serve as an introduction to color on the computer, as well as the current state of digital output for artists.

Color can be measured and translated into mathematical, optical quantities. And that's what a scanner does when scanning your original into a computer workstation. It's also what happens when creating art on a computer workstation; colors are specific and quantified in numerical relationship with other colors. And this quantification is used by the computer when feeding data to another computer, another software program, or to an output device.

Working with color is different on the computer than when using paint. Depending upon the mode in which the computer is operating, or calibrated, all of the color images are created using a combination of red, green, and blue (RGB), or cyan, magenta, and yellow (CMY) projected light. As you know exceedingly well by now, the colors achieved in paint and painting come as a result of light reflected from particles or pigments, each of which has unique physical and optical properties.

Neither system is better than the other; they are merely different. But going from one to the other poses some challenges, as you well know if you've ever tried to scan your original artwork, view it on the screen, and then print it on your desktop printer. The secret to accurate translation from paint color to printed color is in the quality and calibration of the equipment. And, if your goal is highly accurate output of scanned originals, you're

"Starcase" by Cherish Flieder, working in Adobe Illustrator 8.0.

often better off (at least at the time this is being written) enlisting the help of a competent service bureau or output professional.

Permanent Output

It's fair to say that, over the last few years, manufacturers of desktop printers have had to take a crash course in permanence. The first color desktop printers were intended to make flashy pie charts and halfway-decent overheads. Then, as artists and photographers found that the clarity of the image was getting close to photographic, the whole game changed. Suddenly, creative-types were clamoring to find out how long the ink would remain lightfast. And whether or not the paper would remain stable. People from companies like Epson and Canon were hearing questions they'd never before dreamed of.

And the answers weren't all that satisfactory. Wilhelm Imaging Research is a firm that specializes in the measurement of fading, staining, and general stability of hard copy digital and photographic output. The company has done benchmark work in determining the stability of output from a wide range of devices, and its work showed that early ink jet printers, with early inks, were producing output that, in many cases, began to fade or yellow in less than a year.

But things are changing. Dramatically. While low-cost desktop printers still don't produce output that can qualify as permanent and suitable for artists' use (if we go by the category I and II standards established by the ASTM subcommittee on artists' materials), they are getting better. By the time this book is published, the Epson Photo 870 and 1270 printers should be on the market. Using Epson inks, and on Epson Heavyweight Matte Paper, these printers have been rated by Wilhelm Imaging as producing output that will remain stable (under normal conditions) for between twenty-four and twenty-six years.

And things are even better for wide-format ink jet output. The HP Design Jet 2500/3500 CP printers, using HP pigmented ink, have been rated as producing output that will remain stable (under normal conditions) for in excess of two hundred years on Arches Hot Press Paper.

It's important to note that the stability of the output is dependent upon both the ink and the paper substrate. In a paper entitled "The Intimate Relationships of Inks and Papers: You Can't Talk About the Permanence of One Without Considering the Other," Henry Wilhelm notes that, "with a given inkset, the difference in light fading rates between the longest-lasting paper and the least stable paper can exceed 20 to 1. That is, the amount of fading that will take place in 20 years with the best paper can occur in only one year—or even less—with the worst!"

The bottom line? For the most stable and lightfast output, whether you're reproducing original art, or creating hard copy of images created in a purely digital environment, get a little advance information. On the World Wide Web, at www.wilhelm-research.com, you'll find detailed information and tables that identify the most permanent combination of printers, inks, and substrates. And when you're shopping for output, use that information to ensure that you get the permanence you want.

The Art of Early Adopting

Early adopters share two things in common: one, we like new toys and two, we're looking for new solutions. Of the two, the interest in toys is fun but also more than a little superficial (okay, and maybe even a bit juvenile), while the passion for new solutions is enduring. No matter how much fun the new toy is, it won't find a permanent place in our creative arsenal unless it meets a legitimate need.

So, what electronic innovations are on the horizon and that have the potential to alter the face of the art and creative community? Here are five:

The World Wide Web

The Web is changing everything, and I don't believe its impact and importance can be overstated. For the art community, the implications range from great and easy presentation of traditional media (like on the gallery site www.nextmonet.com), to dynamic cyber-communities, like that facilitated for art educators by the Getty Center (at www.artsednet.getty.edu), to art that is developed by individuals or as collaborative exercises, exclusively in cyberspace.

Digital Cameras

At the time of this writing, digital cameras are costly (compared to film-based cameras), the picture quality isn't as good, and output is limited. But that's changing rapidly. Early adopters have already embraced digital cameras and it won't be long before we see new cameras that are cost-competitive, offer spectacular picture quality, and that present a wide array of easy output options via low-cost computers and printers. That may be the last hurdle needed for the average twenty-first century creative-type to fully discard the view of computers as daunting and mysterious, and begin viewing them as fun, responsive art-making stations.

"Cherished Memories," by Cherish Flieder. This piece combines digital illustration with traditional painting. Completed in Adobe Photoshop 5.5.

Increased Output Permanence

If I'm certain of anything, it's that all of the elements discussed above—printers, inks and dyes, and output substrates—will continue to evolve. It won't be long before we see inexpensive desktop printers producing output that will last a solid century or two.

An Integrated Color System

There has never before been a color system that fully integrates the language of color in common usage by artists with a graphic arts color specification system used for printing with a color specification system used on computers. But things are looking up.

Jean Bourges recently published a stunning book called *Color Bytes* (Chromatics Press, 1997) that outlines a simple, well-conceived system for using color within any of the three environments listed above. The Bourges system works equally well for painters as it does for art students as it does for printers as it does for graphic artists and computer-types.

If the name sounds familiar, Jean Bourges started a company in 1947 with her father, Albert Bourges, to make and market Bourges Color Sheets. The sheets, and the family, were responsible for a color revolution in the middle part of this century. Now, as if one color revolution wasn't enough, Jean is bringing her original contribution to an elegant, symmetrical conclusion.

Pen Computing

My one-pound Newton computer has a simple, easy-to-use drawing program included that allows me to sketch directly on the screen (you should see the sketch of my daughter and her dog that opens every time the system starts up). The Newton is more powerful—and the software easier to use—than the original desktop Macintosh. And we all know where that led.

Ignore the recent fate of the Newton (which was discontinued by Apple not long after its introduction). The technology won't disappear, and it points to some remarkable developments on the horizon. Just look at the remarkable success of the PalmPilot handheld computer and the commitment made by Microsoft with its Windows CE operating system to the pen-based computer market.

What's it all mean? If pen-based computing travels a path half as dynamic as that taken by personal computers, we'll see lightweight, handheld computer pads in a few short years that allow us to draw, paint, and import photographic images, all with great precision and ease. All of this in full-blown color and at low cost. We'll be able to use these pads as easily as we now pick up a pad of sketch paper and a pencil. We'll be able to view images on the computer pad of historical, annotated artwork next to our own cataloged drawings and paintings.

How close is this scenario? A handful of talented engineers at MIT are working on paper-thin computer displays that can be bound into a book or pad (*WIRED Magazine*, "Digital Ink," May 1997). I wouldn't bet against them.

What will this revolution mean for traditional materials and traditional artists? I wish I could say. The computer is, without doubt, an astonishing and exhilarating tool. Will it completely supplant oils, acrylics, and watercolors on traditional surfaces? For some, it will. For others, the computer will be integrated into the studio as one of many tools, some new and some old. And, for still others, I suspect that there's not an electronic substitute for the tactile and sensual reward that comes with pencil and brush in hand. How the final mix will evolve, I'm not ready to guess. But it sure will be interesting to watch.

With all of this talk about electronic gadgets and gizmos, I don't want to be mistaken for one who has abandoned his roots as an art materials romantic. I simply believe that, more than ever before, being an artist in the twenty-first century will require an open mind and a willingness to integrate new tools with traditional materials.

Let me say right here that I love my size-12, handmade Winsor & Newton Series 7 Kolinsky watercolor brush every bit as much as I love my Macintosh laptop computer. I love how the brush feels in my hand, and how it feels on the painting surface. Now if someone could just figure out how I can project digital video from the brush handle—I'd buy THAT in a World Wide Web minute!

Chapter 7

Don't Hold Your Breath! Health and Safety

In the summer and fall of 1999, Duane Slick got a rude awakening. Slick is the current chair of the painting department with the Rhode Island School of Design (RISD), and he found that the Environmental Protection Agency (EPA) had made visits to neighboring universities, looking for environmental hazardous waste. What's more, Slick found that the EPA had identified schools and universities as possible "waste generators" and as a priority for investigation. Uh oh.

All of a sudden, all of that paint and pigment and solvent that, up to now, had been a health and safety concern for students just within the immediate studio environment, took on a whole new dimension. What was happening to all of that stuff going down the drain? And why was the EPA targeting schools?

To make a long story short, RISD hired an independent consultant that was well-versed in waste regulations to help them head off the EPA at the pass. Slick and the school staff learned about some specific issues (that I'll detail shortly), and they also learned something bigger: "There are personal health and safety issues with using these materials," says Slick, "and there are environmental issues. And we've found out that you really can't separate the two. They really are two sides of the same coin."

The point to this discussion—the bottom line, as I've been fond of saying many times during the writing of this book—is that the use of art materials can and should be as safe as any activity on the planet. (Not to mention the fact that using them makes you feel so good.) But they do require care and some knowledge.

The real issue is in identifying which of the products and materials can, during normal use, find entry into your body. And, once they get there, can they cause systemic problems?

While this discussion is not meant to alarm artists, it is intended to impress upon you that—while the vast majority of products used in your studio are inert and innocuous—some require special attention. And that all materials should be used with respect.

Before outlining some safe studio practices, here are a few issues, brought to light by the EPA's recent interest in school environs, that are worth reporting:

• The EPA has identified eight metals, or elements, that have the potential to be a health concern. Those are: arsenic, barium, cadmium, chromium, lead, mercury, selenium, and silver. These elements, the "RCRA 8" (which sounds like a band of revolutionaries from the '60s), are closely monitored by the agency. And some of them are found in pigments used in the manufacture of art materials.

• Once the products have been identified that contain the metals in question, the solubility of the metals within those pigments has to be measured. Why? Because the element poses a risk only if it can be absorbed into the human system or the environment. If it's largely insoluble, then it poses little or no concern. So, the EPA has identified certain solubility levels below which the pigment or product is not considered a danger or as hazardous waste. Above that level, and the product requires special disposal provisions.

• Solubility is tested through something called the "Toxicity Characteristic Leaching Procedure" (TCLP). TCLP testing determines how much of a given metal goes into solution within a specific acid environment. For example, if, during the course of testing a compound or pigment containing cadmium, greater that 1 milligram of cadmium per liter (1 mg/l) of solution shows up, the compound in question is considered to be hazardous waste. The limits for lead and chromium is 5 mg/l. If the solubility of the element is less than the EPA limit, the product is not considered to require special treatment.

• In an attempt to be proactive, RISD requested solubility testing from art material manufacturers on all products that contain any of the RCRA 8 metals. Armed with that data, RISD was prepared to say that any materials being used in the studios contained either nothing more than trace amounts of the metals or contained metal-containing compounds that were below the solubility threshold as defined by the EPA.
• The vast majority of the products used at RISD (and at other schools as well as in your studio) were shown to include either none of the RCRA 8 metals or to have solubility levels well below the EPA limits.

That's good news. Art material manufacturers have been trying for years to use products and pigments of lesser and lesser solubility. The result is colors that pose minimal risk. Note, however, the word "minimal." While most cadmium-containing products have been measured at solubility levels well below the EPA limits, it's very difficult to test these products in a manner that exactly replicates the environment found within your stomach and mine. Or within our lungs, if we're spray-applying a color or compound. So, while all of this is good news, these products still require some care.

And, while the vast majority of products does not exceed the EPA limits, there are some products that do. Some colors made by a variety of manufacturers contain chromium that exceeds the TCLP limits by amounts that range from very small to moderate. And any oil color containing lead will exceed the TCLP limits by a large degree. Does this mean that those colors shouldn't be used? It's up to you. If used, however, they clearly should be with care and caution (see Safe Studio Practices below).

The situation at RISD is continuing to evolve. I'm sure that these issues will come to the fore at other schools and institutions in the near future. And forewarned is forearmed.

So, how can you guard and ensure your safety in the studio?

Safe Studio Practices

Remember that there are short-term effects as well as long-term, or cumulative, effects that can arise from the improper use of these materials. So, just because you don't notice anything of concern right now, it doesn't mean that, ten years down the road, you won't get a nasty surprise if you've been using materials improperly. So, these practices should apply all of the time, to all products, not just a chosen few.

Some Essential Pointers

• **Always read the product labels.** The labeling standard for Chronic Health Hazards in Art Materials (ASTM D-4236) has been codified into US law as part of the Federal Hazardous Substances Act 15 USC S 1277. In cooperation with the Art & Creative Materials Institute (ACMI), all art and creative products marketed in the USA include labeling that details if and how precautions should be taken. So, if there's a concern, you'll see it on the label.

In addition, the American Society for Testing and Materials (ASTM) has prepared standards for the safe use of artists' materials. These have been published as a booklet entitled "ASTM Standards for the Performance, Quality, and Health Labeling of Artists' Paints and Related Materials," ISBN 0-8031-1838-4. The address for ASTM is: ASTM, 100 Barr Harbor Drive, West Conshohocken, PA 19428-2959.

The standards used for the safe use of artists' materials in the US are different than those used in European countries. If you have questions about European standards and labeling on specific products, contact the manufacturer.

When Working,

• **Always make sure that there's plenty of fresh air and ventilation.** Gamblin Artists Colors suggests placing a small box fan in one window, and opening another to ensure adequate air exchange, positioning in the working area so that any vapors move from the painting table or easel directly to the window—and not across the artist.

• **If spray applying any products, wear an approved mask.** A spray booth or, even better, an extraction system, vented to the outside is recommended.

• **If working with powdered pigment, the above provisions for ventilation are even more important.** I once worked with an artist who was applying pure pigment using an electrostatic process. And he worked without adequate ventilation. It wasn't but a few years before his kidneys failed as a result. Thank goodness, with careful medical treatment, he recovered. But the lesson is clear: Applying any product or pigment that can become airborne requires appropriate ventilation.

• **Always keep all materials, especially solvents, tightly sealed.** This means keeping the threads on lids and jars wiped clean, to ensure a better seal when closed.

- **Art materials should never be exposed to heat sources or to naked flame.**
- **Do not eat, drink, or smoke when working.** You never know what may end up on your fingers, your food, or your cigarette, and then get swallowed inadvertently.
- **Avoid skin contact, particularly with solvents. Don't paint directly with your fingers.**
- **Wherever and whenever possible, use a low-aromatic solvent**, such as **Sansodor** from Winsor & Newton, or **Gamsol** from Gamblin Artists Colors. Both have equal Threshold Limit Values (TLV, at 300 ppm) and, of the two, Sansodor has a slightly higher and safer flash point.
- **Avoid turpentine, wherever possible.** Turpentine is a proven health hazard for many, and it can be absorbed directly through the skin. This means that any pigment on your hands, if combined with turpentine, will be carried through your skin and into your system, as well.
- **Don't wash or rinse brushes in the palm of your hand.** Doing so, particularly if laden with solvent, is a particularly efficient method for driving pigment into and through your skin.
- **When washing brushes or palettes or other tools…**
  - First, wipe them free of color with a paper towel. If using stiff brushes with thick color, like oils or acrylics, an old toothbrush works well for scraping free excess color. Allow the product on the towel to dry completely before disposal.
  - Rinse the brush or tool free of color with a minimum amount of low-aromatic solvent. If working in watercolor or acrylic, rinse with water.
  - Wash the brush with a conditioning soap.
  - Never store brushes resting in a container head, or tuft, down.
  - If looking to eliminate all solvents from your studio, consider using water-mixable oils.
- **Do not point your brushes in your mouth.** I don't know how many times I've watched people in studios, classrooms, and art stores stick a brush in their mouths, looking for a fine point. Bad idea. Swirl the brush in a cup of water, or solvent, to check the point.
- **If using solvent, pour out only as much as needed for your current painting session.** Too much open solvent means solvent vapor in your immediate environment.

- **SMALL AMOUNTS of LOW-AROMATIC solvent can be allowed to evaporate in a well-ventilated area** rather than being disposed of down the sink. Note: Low-aromatic means solvents with a high TLV (such as Sansodor from Winsor & Newton, or Gamsol from Gamblin Artists Colors; both have TLVs at 300 ppm). This does NOT include more heavily aromatic solvents like turpentine.
- **Excess solvents can be disposed of at your local recycling center.**
- As a safeguard for groundwater, do not dispose of excess oil or acrylic color or solvent down the sink. Instead, use the following guidelines:
- **When finished painting with acrylic colors, allow waste paint and paper towels to fully dry before disposal.** Why? Because the dried polymer vehicle will provide some containment for the included pigment, minimizing the risk of solubility in landfills and waste water. Then discard the resulting solids.
- When finished painting with oil colors, gather up all solvent and paint-laden rags, as well as any discarded palettes. Allow the rags and waste material to dry in a well-ventilated area (outdoors is a good place, if protected from excessive wind, or from children and pets). Dispose of them in an airtight, solvent-proof container.
- Lead-based colors, or any solvents used with lead-based colors, should never be disposed of in household trash or down the drain.
- **For disposal recommendations and regulations pertaining to all art materials, as well as more toxic solvents, aerosol cans, and highly toxic pigments (like lead-based colors)**, contact The Center for Safety in the Arts at NYFA at www.artswire.org:70/1/csa/ or 155 Avenue of the Americas, 14th Floor, New York, NY, 10013.
- **If paint or solvent is somehow splashed in your eyes, flush immediately and thoroughly with cold water.**
- **Clean up all spills immediately.**
- **Unless specifically labeled as safe for children's use, keep artists' materials away from children.** Because of their lesser size and body weight, youngsters are subject to greater risk with these products than adults. Better to limit their exposure altogether.
- **Give things away.** If left with products or paints you won't be using any more, give them to a friend.

Throw away as little as possible.

• **Spray cans should never be thrown away unless fully emptied.** Before disposing in the trash, spray adhesives, spray fixatives, spray paints, or spray varnishes should be emptied by spraying (outside or in a spray booth) until no residue remains.

• **Wash your hands when you're done!** Again, don't use solvent. Wipe any color or excess materials from your hands with a paper towel. A good soap or hand cleaner should be perfectly adequate for a thorough cleansing.

• **When traveling with oil colors, avoid carrying products with a flash point below 61 centigrade.** Materials with a low flash point are considered Group II or Group III flammable materials, and are considered unsuitable for airline travel. In general, those products include:

• Oil color solvents (except **Sansodor**, from Winsor & Newton, which has a flash point of 70C, and **Gamsol**, from Gamblin Artists Colors, with a flash point of 63C)

• Oil color mediums

• Oil color varnishes

There are a number of oil color products that are within allowable flash point limits (consult the manufacturer). Winsor & Newton has published a list of its oil products that are suitable for travel. Other manufacturers should be able to provide you with similar information. And carry the documented information when traveling. You never know when you may need to offer documentation to an intransigent airline official.

• A word about **gloves**: There are times when impermeable gloves are clearly worth using. But, because of potential allergic reactions and other serious toxicity considerations, it's wise to eschew the use of gloves made of latex. In particular, latex gloves powdered for easy donning and removal should be avoided. Why? Because snapping those gloves off and on, as almost always happens, means that the latex-laden powder ends up in the air and is breathable. A better choice, and one currently being used at RISD, is a more inert nitrile glove call **Ambti-dex**.

Notice that I've not specified any special precautions for colors containing cadmium or chromium or the other RCRA 8 metals. That's because, if you follow the above procedures, you'll be insulating yourself and others from exposure to all potentially hazardous materials, not just the few that have been presently identified as being of concern. And, to be safe, all materials should be treated with the same degree of care. Prescribing different levels of precaution, for different colors, is a sure route to confusion and eventual exposure. It's better to establish safe practices with all materials!

There are a number of other highly detailed resources regarding studio safety. And it's worth repeating here that specific information about procedures, regulations, and practical tips on things like choosing the right protective glove or respirator is available from The Center for Safety in the Arts at NYFA (see page 137 for the address).

Other books and resources regarding health and safety are listed in the next chapter.

Chapter 8
There's More?
Other Resources

Trying to pack this much information into a book of this size is like trying to jam an elephant into a gelcap. There's simply too much great chemistry, history, and information about specific applications to get into one volume. This book has been intended to give you a solid foundation and to ensure that you'll be able to recognize when you're faced with a situation requiring more detailed information.

While not exhaustive, this list of additional resources is a solid start for anyone interested in tracking down more information about a wide range of subject matter.

Books
Painting and General Reference

Bourges, Jean. *Color Bytes*. New York: Chromatics Press. 1997.
A book that systematically integrates color theory for painters, graphic designers, and computer-types. A wonderful and much-needed reference.

Gettens, Rutherford and George Stout. *Painting Materials: A Short Encyclopedia*, 2nd Edition. New York: Dover Publications. 1966. Originally published in 1942 by D. Van Nostrand.
I wasn't kidding when I said that I carry this book in my brief bag all of the time. It's compact and has the best collection of obscure chemical and technical information available.

Gottsegen, Mark. *The Painter's Handbook*. New York: Watson Guptill. 1993.
This outstanding reference has a great deal of detailed information, by a terrifically dedicated individual.

Mayer, Ralph. *A Dictionary of Art Terms and Techniques*, 2nd Edition. New York: Harper Collins. 1991.

– *The Artist's Handbook on Materials and Techniques*, 5th Edition, revised by Steven Sheehan. New York: Viking. 1991. Originally published in 1941.
Long considered to be the art material "bible."

Pearce, Emma. *Artists' Materials: Which, Why and How*. London: A&C Black. 1992.
A superb, very compact, and exceedingly well-organized reference.

Saitzyk, Steven. *Art Hardware*. New York: Watson Guptill. 1987.
A very readable text that offers much useable information.

Smith, Ray. *The Artist's Handbook*. New York: Alfred A. Knopf. 1989.
Beautifully illustrated; well-organized with excellent information regarding materials and techniques. Comprehensive and easy-to-read pigment tables beginning on page 18. This book is a dandy.

Wehlte, Kurt. *The Materials and Techniques of Painting*. New York: Van Nostrand Reinhold. 1975.

Brushes

Turner, Jacques. *Brushes: A Handbook for Artists and Artisans*. New York: Design Press. 1992.
This terrific little manual is an easy read. It's loaded with helpful information and written by someone who cares greatly about his subject.

Paper

Hunter, Dard. *Papermaking: The History and Technique of an Ancient Craft*. New York: Dover Publications. 1943.
A wonderful and fun read for anyone interested in the history and romance of paper. Hunter is considered to be the "father" of twentieth century western hand papermaking.

Long, Paulette, ed. *Paper: Art and Technology*. San Francisco: World Print Council. 1979.
An outstanding introduction to the technical issues regarding papermaking.

Toale, Bernard. *The Art of Papermaking*. Massachusetts: Davis Publications. 1983.
Maybe the best introduction to making paper by hand.

Turner, Sylvie. *Which Paper? A Guide to Choosing and Using Fine Papers*. New York: Design Press. 1992.
What a lovely and welcome book this is. Well-written and beautifully designed, this text should be mandatory for every art material professional and every artist who uses paper.

Hazards

McCann, Michael. *Artist Beware*. New York: Watson Guptill. 1979.
Aside from the "horror movie" title, this is a helpful reference.

— *Health Hazards Manual for Artists*. New York: Lyons and Burford. 1985.
This book lists chemical hazards first and then the products in which they may be found. The section "Hazards of Various Media," starting on page 26, offers much useful information.

Spandorfer, Merle, Deborah Curtiss, and Jack Snyder, MD. *Making Art Safely*. New York: Van Nostrand Reinhold. 1993.
Hardbound and nicely illustrated, this book offers comprehensive, detailed information about health and safety in painting, printmaking, photography, graphic design, and just about every art-making environment imaginable.

On the World Wide Web

ArtsWire
www.artswire.org
A terrific site that includes information for artists in a wide range of areas. Includes a comprehensive listing of links to related sites and organizations in the arts.

ArtsEdNet with the Getty Center
www.artsednet.getty.edu
A superb resource for art educators and institutions. Includes lesson plans, galleries and exhibitions, a chat venue, and more.

The Center for Safety in the Arts at NYFA
www.artswire.org:70/1/csa/
The most comprehensive site on the web for detailed information about health and safety.

Wilhelm Imaging Research
www.wilhelm-research.com
This is the site that details current research regarding stability and permanence of electronic printing and output. For those of you making art on computers, this is a site worth bookmarking and checking every few months.

Winsor & Newton
www.winsornewton.com
A huge, encyclopedic site that has been recognized for its excellent level of organization, its visual appeal, and the quality of information. There is a complete encyclopedia section, as well as sections that detail how to get started with various media, comprehensive tips and techniques, unusual applications, and more.

Gamblin Artists Colors
www.gamblincolors.com
A beautifully designed site that reflects the personal qualities of the manufacturer. Excellent information on studio safety and painting techniques, as well as the history of colors.

Golden Artist Colors
www.goldenartistcolors.com
Over the last twenty years, Golden has done a remarkable job in presenting detailed technical information, and the company's web site is a product of that same expertise.

Liquitex
www.liquitex.com
A site that includes excellent technical information in combination with features about artists and students using acrylic colors in a variety of ways.

Index

single pigment 42, 44
sinking 56
solvent 53, 55, 112, 137
spectrum 40
spray cans 138
stable film 50
staining colors 80
stand oil 74
Starr, Susanna
    "PRESS 1999" 118
Stout, George L. 71
student-grade colors 64, 70
synthetic iron oxide 38, 40
synthetic organic pigments 80

T
Tate Gallery 123
tempera 17, 125
testing color 72-73
thick underlayers of color 113
threshold limit value (TLV) 55
Titanium White 79
Toxicity Characteristic Leaching
    Procedure (TCLP) 135
traditional colors 80-81
transparency 77
Transparent Yellow (Azo) 79
triple-roll mill 46-48
turpentine 55, 137
Tyrian purple 29

U
Uccello, Paolo
    "The Battle of San Romano in
    1432" 15
ultraviolet 59
underbound 73
underbound color 54
underpainting 112, 114

with acrylics 112
Underpainting White 104
undertone 75
ultramarine blue 19

V
van Eyck, Jan
    "The Arnolfini Wedding" 16-17,
    75
varnish 115, 123, 125
varnishing (oils, how to) 114
    testing for readiness 114
    temporary 115
    isolating 115
    retouching 115
vehicle 81
    function of 91
    stability of 81
Vermeer, Johannes
    "Girl with the Red Hat" 32, 102
Vermilion 14, 32, 64
viewing palette 108

W
water molecules 89
watercolor 84
    brushes for 99-101
        camel hair 101
        brushmaking 100
        flow control 100
        Kolinsky 101
        Petit Gris 101
        sabeline 101
        sable 101
        squirrel 101
        synthetic 101
    bugs 59
    framing 101-102
    mediums for 99

blending medium 99
    granulation medium 99
    iridescent medium 99
    lifting preparation 99
    permanent masking medium 99
    texture medium 99
paper 94-97
    absorbancy of 97
    acid-free 95
    cold press 94
    deckle edge 95
    durability of 97
    formation of 95
    hot press 94
    laid 95
    permanence of 97
    pH neutral 95
    rough 94
    sizing of 95
    stretching of 97
    tooth 95
    watermark 95
    weight of 95
    wove 95
    transparent 92
well-milled paint 46
Wilhelm Imaging Research 132
Winsor, William 90
World Wide Web 132

X
x-rays 59
xenon-arc fadeometer 71

Y
Yellow Ochre 80

Z
Zinc White 79